Effective Communication and Engagement with Children and Young People, Their Families and Carers

Creating Integrated Services – titles in the series

To order other titles from Learning Matters, please contact our distributors:
BEBC Distribution, Albion Close, Parkstone, Poole, BH12 3LL. Telephone: 0845 230 9000,
email: learningmatters@bebc.co.uk

You can find more information on our titles and other learning resources at
www.learningmatters.co.uk

Effective Communication and Engagement with Children and Young People, Their Families and Carers

Edited by

ALLY DUNHILL,

BARBARA ELLIOTT

and

ANGELA SHAW

Series Editors: Jonathan Parker and Greta Bradley

First published 2009 by Learning Matters Ltd
Reprinted in 2010

© Ally Dunhill, Barbara Elliott, Kyriaki Messiou, Angela Shaw, Eileen Wake and Clare Whitfield, 2009

British Library Cataloguing in Publication Data
A CIP record for this book is available from the British Library

ISBN: 978 1 84445 265 1

The right of Ally Dunhill, Barbara Elliott, Kyriaki Messiou, Angela Shaw, Eileen Wake and Clare Whitfield to be identified as the Authors of this Work has been asserted by them in accordance with the Copyright, Designs and Patents Act 1988.

Cover design by Code 5 Design Associates
Text design by Code 5 Design Associates
Project Management by Swales & Willis Ltd, Exeter, Devon
Typeset by Kelly Gray
Printed and bound in Great Britain by TJ International Ltd, Padstow, Cornwall

Learning Matters Ltd
33 Southernhay East
Exeter EX1 1NX
Tel: 01392 215560
E-mail: info@learningmatters.co.uk
www.learningmatters.co.uk

Contents

About the authors

Ally Dunhill is a lecturer in early years and interprofessional studies and programme director for the BA Children's Interprofessional Studies at the University of Hull. She has spent 20 years working in a range of establishments and organisations for children, young people and their families. Her experiences include working with 0–4 year olds in the private sector, 5–18 year olds in mainstream schools and those aged 16 years and over in further and higher education.

Angela Shaw after a long career in education as a teacher, youth and community worker, and lecturer in both FE and HE, Angela is now Head of Centre for Educational Studies in the Institute for Learning at the University of Hull. She teaches on both undergraduate and postgraduate programmes and has published in academic journals in the last two years.

Barbara Elliott is a lecturer in the Faculty of Health and Social Care and co-director of the Inter-professional Services Centre for Children, Young People and Families at the University of Hull. A children's nurse by background, she teaches on a range of pro-grammes, including the undergraduate child nursing courses and the BA Children's Inter-professional Studies degree. She has conducted research and published papers on a number of aspects of child health, including physical activity, chronic illness and naso-gastric feeding.

Kyriaki Messiou is currently a lecturer in Education, in the Centre for Educational Studies, at the University of Hull. She teaches and supervises undergraduate and postgraduate students in Special and Inclusive Education. She has worked as a school teacher and as a special education teacher in primary mainstream schools in Cyprus. She gained a MEd in Special Education, a MSc in Educational Research and a PhD in Inclusive Education, from the University of Manchester. Her research interests cover the area of inclusive education and, in particular, exploring children's voices to understand notions of marginalisation and inclusive practices in education. She has published articles in peer-reviewed academic journals and has presented papers at international conferences.

Eileen Wake is a paediatric nurse lecturer at the University of Hull. She has worked within children's and learning disability nursing services for the past 25 years, the past 13 of which have been based within the University of Hull, and with children's specialist services in the local health care trust. Her specialist areas of interest are children and young people with complex health needs and/or life-limiting conditions, as well as ethical and legal aspects of child health and social care. Her publications have mainly focused on caring for people with profound and multiple disabilities and related complex health care needs, as well as the emotional well-being of children and young people, includ-ing emotional intelligence, resilience and resultant issues/problems in relation to mental health needs. She is currently developing a website focusing upon consent in relation to health, education and social care when working with children, young people and their families.

Clare Whitfield works as a research associate in the Faculty of Health and Social Care Department at the University of Hull. She also teaches in the faculties of Social Sciences and Education. Clare is a registered nurse with a research interest in empowerment and the maintenance of autonomy amongst patients within the National Health Service. She has worked as an associate lecturer at the University of Hull since 2001.

Acknowledgements

We, the editors, would like to thank all our colleagues at the University of Hull for their support in the compilation of this book, both those who have directly contributed chapters and those who have offered friendly criticism. We would particularly like to thank Jackie Lison for her help in getting the book into good shape in the hurried final stages.

We would like to dedicate the book with love to our respective offspring: Fraser, Lucy, Louise, Laura, Stuart, Kieron, Jody and Bronwen. These are the people who have given us so much direct personal experience of engagement and communication with children, and within families, in our own lives.

Introduction

This book has been written by staff at the University of Hull, drawn from the Institute for Learning and the Faculty of Health and Social Care. Teams of staff from these two faculties have been working together with colleagues from Social Work for several years to develop new initiatives in children's inter-professional studies. The team has developed new programmes of study, for example BA (Hons) Children's Inter-professional Studies, alongside a centre for the support of practitioners and a centre for multidisciplinary research.

The book addresses the needs of those who are studying and working in the new integrated children's services sector and is a must-read for anyone working within inter-professional settings engaging with children, young people, their families and carers. It focuses on providing information and guidance for those who are involved in the newly emerging multi-agency, interdisciplinary children's workforce by helping them to develop strategies for communication and engagement with children, their families and carers.

The government's policies, as encapsulated in *Every Child Matters* and *Youth Matters*, produced in response to the Laming Report into the death of Victoria Climbié, have heralded a substantial change in the last three years in the organisation of children's services in the UK. Teachers, social workers, health professionals, youth workers and care workers are all now expected to combine their working practices and strategies to provide holistic care for children and families.

This has led to the creation of Departments of Children's Services across the country, replacing former Local Education Authorities and Social Services Children's Divisions. It has also demanded a new set of workforce standards (the Common Core of Competences for the Children's Workforce), and a new Common Assessment Framework for identifying and supporting children at risk or in need. These policies and new procedures underpin the need for this book at this time.

Current government initiatives are also aimed at giving children and young people a real say in the services that affect them. For example, the Department of Health has demonstrated commitment in involving children in its work through the publication of its action plan: *Listening, hearing and responding*: *Core principles for the involvement of children and young people* (DoH, 2002a). More recently, the Children's Society involved children and young people in their research for *The Good Childhood Inquiry* (Layard and Dunn, 2009). This study of the current state of childhood in Britain clearly shows that children and young people in Britain experience more mental and physical ill health than those in other European countries and that many young people feel marginalised and excluded by their communities. Comments from young people indicate that adults' and society's attitudes towards them, including issues of respect and fairness, are important and influence their quality of life. The publication of this book supports such initiatives and responds to the concerns of young people by giving practitioners clear skills to ensure that the voices of children, young people and their families are heard when delivering services and their views respected.

As the new government agenda for children and young people develops, it is being supported by the emergence of new undergraduate and postgraduate programmes across the UK, all designed to provide the inter-professional children's workforce for the future. This book provides a rich source of material for these students and their teachers/trainers, as well as being a useful resource for those already working in the sector.

For those readers studying at undergraduate level the book is a core text providing guidance and information, including ways to link theory and practice through case studies and exercises. The book provides childcare workers already involved in the newly emerging multi-agency, interdisciplinary children's workforce with information to develop their understanding of the theory behind the issues relating to communication and engagement in multi-agency settings for children and families. In addition, readers are enabled to develop strategies for effective communication and engagement with children, their families and carers. Suggested further reading and a comprehensive bibliography direct the reader to the wide range of literature and research in this area.

This book:

- Provides examples of strategies for communication and engagement with children, young people, their families and carers.

- Supports preparation for work in the new integrated children's services sector for those at the start of their studies in this area.

- Provides information and guidance for those who are involved in the newly emerging multi-agency, interdisciplinary children's workforce, who are undertaking professional development or training to enhance understanding and skills.

Below is a summary of the chapters in this book, each of which addresses key issues relating to communicating with children, young people and families. Chapters 1 to 3 focus on the context of communication, while Chapters 4 to 6 consider specific issues relating to the diverse settings and child and family needs that childcare workers encounter. The final chapter focuses on the legal and ethical dimensions of communication with children, young people and their families.

Effective communication is essential in meeting current policy aims. Communication is central to all interactions between people. This includes encounters between service users seeking support and professional practitioners, as well as between practitioners themselves and the agencies they represent. Chapter 1 reviews the historical policy context and explores current policy support for adequate communication in relation to new empowering practices for managing individual cases, the promotion of inter-professional collaboration and inter-agency working.

Chapter 2 starts with a definition of communication and aims to develop an understanding of the process in which children and young people, adults and families transfer information. It explores the theories, methods and levels of engagement in communication. Central to this chapter is the developmental process of communication and how it transforms and transmits to all areas of life: the home environment, at school, within the community, at work and within work and beyond.

Chapter 3 explores the concept of listening to children's voices in order to truly make every child matter. First, it explores how children's voices were absent in the past and how a greater emphasis has been placed on children's voices in recent years in various countries, especially after the UN Convention on the Rights of the Child (UNICEF, 1989). Particular reference is made to the national context and the emphasis given to children's voices through the *Every Child Matters* (DfES, 2003) agenda. The importance of listening to children's voices is analysed using examples from research, both in the UK and overseas, to illustrate, on the one hand, various practical ways of engaging with children's voices and, on the other, the importance of doing so. The main focus is on education, with particular emphasis on practices related to inclusive education that aim to make sure that every child does matter. The different ways to engage with children's voices presented can be used across disciplines to effectively communicate with children. Finally, some of the difficulties associated with the issue of listening to children's voices are discussed.

Chapter 4 looks at the importance of listening for, not just to, children. It explores emotional intelligence, resilience and vulnerability and considers communicating with children and young people to promote emotional well-being. Communication with children under pressure, vulnerable children and young people, and those with mental health needs are explored, including children with ASD and sensory impairment. Central to this chapter is the importance of multi-sensory communication for all children with learning disabilities. Augmentative communication, body signs, Makaton, communication technologies and resources to enhance practice are described. The chapter concludes with an opportunity for the reader to reflect on their own current communication approaches, limits and scope and identify their own future developmental needs.

Chapter 5 re-emphasises the importance of communication within the family and presents an overview of the different settings, outside the family home, in which children and young people may find themselves. These include schools, nurseries, childminders' homes, in kinship or foster care, and residential institutions connected with education, youth justice or behavioural issues. The chapter examines the particular issues for communication and engagement with families and children where care is provided on day care and residential bases. The chapter addresses the challenges of building rapport and trust with children and young people who are in unfamiliar settings, who have continual disruption through changes in setting, who have had negative experiences of day care, residential or foster care and/or have low levels of resilience. It also looks at how good communication and positive engagement can be used with families and carers to promote the best quality of life for the children and adults involved in the care process.

Chapter 6 explores the importance of effective communication and engagement with children, young people and families in health care contexts. The evidence regarding inter-actions between health care professionals and children, young people and families is reviewed and recommendations for good practice made. Consideration is given to the role of communication in promoting positive health choices and facilitating access to appro-priate health care for children and young people. The role of communication in preparing children for health care encounters, including hospitalisation, is discussed with regard to facilitating understanding and encouraging emotional rehearsal and expression. Play as a communication tool, including therapeutic play, is explored in health care contexts. Effective communication with parents and families, including siblings, is discussed with particular regard to supporting parents after the delivery of complex medical information or diagnosis of serious conditions and illness. Communicating with families during bereavement is explored, including helping children and young people facing life-limiting conditions. The chapter concludes with a summary of the key issues to consider when communicating with children, young people and families in health care contexts, their specific needs for communication, and the evidence-based, effective strategies available.

Chapter 7 explores the rights of children and young people and the resultant implications for practitioners in relation to communication. A wide range of areas is considered, including children and young people's right to confidentiality and advocacy. An important dimension in working with children and young people is allowing them to make their own decisions regarding care and medical treatment. Therefore the duty of care for practitioners to empower and support children and young people in such decision making using a range of communication skills is examined. The needs of children and young people who have limited capacity to express their needs and wishes is explored, as well as the communication skills and knowledge needed in working with children and young people with fluctuating capacity due to health needs. The rights and resultant communication issues related to working in partnership with young people aged 16–17 years are also specifically explored.

In order to enhance understanding of these complex communication issues, a range of legislation, such as the Children Act 1989, 2004, the Mental Capacity Act 2005 and the Mental Health Act 2007, is examined where appropriate and examples provided from case law. The chapter concludes with resources from statutory and non-statutory agencies.

Chapter 1

Communication: The historical and current social policy context

Clare Whitfield

Objectives

By the end of this chapter, you should have an understanding of:

- Changes in focus over the last 30 years and the move away from segregated, agency-determined support provision to the promotion of integrated, client-led services.
- The importance of effective communication in meeting the current policy aims of:
  - Inter-agency working
  - Inter-professional collaboration
  - Client empowerment.

This chapter will look at the link between the wider policy context and its impact on the relationship between the professional and the individual service user. Social policy structures this relationship as it lays out the expectations and roles of both. Changes in policy aims have direct consequences for the type of relationship and therefore the type of communication between professionals and their clients. However, policy itself is shaped by political ideology. The first part of this chapter will look at the links between political ideology and arising social policy. The second part will examine the impact that recent policy has had on communication between professionals and service users.

Introduction

Communication is central to all interactions between people. This includes encounters between agencies that provide welfare and support, between professional practitioners and between professionals and service users seeking support. Communication in a professional environment is governed by social policy, as it is policy that structures the laws, rules and protocols a professional is expected to work within. It defines the role expected of governments, agencies and professional workers, and identifies the rights and responsibilities of individuals.

How communication between different groups is supported in policy reflects differing views of the relationship between the individual and the state and is characterised by differing power dynamics within these. The relationships between agencies, professionals and service users have changed across the last 30 years. In 1979, welfare and support services were state-run and administered by local authorities (LAs). Although services were provided 'in house', paid for and managed by the state, there was minimal interaction between the different agencies that provided welfare services. Professional groups often worked within designated boundaries, with designated roles and within separate spheres. Support available to members of the public was dominated by agency agendas and professional interests, with the individual seen as passive and responsible for following the directions of professionals. In contrast, current policy promotes 'holistic working', supports inter-agency and inter-professional collaboration and includes scope for new empowering practices to support individuals in the management of their own cases.

Changes in social policy impact on communication in professional practice in a number of areas. First, policy defines how communication and working between the available services is achieved; second, it structures rules, protocols and procedures that govern how professionals are expected to interact with one another to provide these services. Third, it contains expectations and assumptions about the roles of both professional workers and those seeking help, including their relationship, which influence the type and level of communication expected between them. Appreciating the social policy context in which professionals work therefore provides a background as to why and how communication is central to service provision. There are two central strands to this discussion: the changes in social policy over the past 30 years and the impact of current policy on professional practice.

Social policy structures the environment in which professionals practice and service users access support. Its aims, and the means mobilised to achieve those aims, however, are shaped by political ideology; these different approaches to social policy result in differences in the range of services that are available and how they are provided. To unpack these links, we will look at the shift apparent over the last 30 years from segregated, agency-determined support provision that frames the service user as a passive receiver of support to the promotion of integrated, client-led services that conceive of the service user as an empowered member of the inter-collaborative team. However, before we explore these issues, we must first define three key concepts: social policy, political ideology and the welfare state.

Social policy

The term social policy has a number of definitions, for example it is an academic discipline; however, in the sense relevant here, it refers to *a set of policies adopted by an organisation to achieve social purposes* (Erskine, 2001, p. 14) as it provides a plan for *social action in the real world* (Alcock et al., 2001, p. 7). The main focus of social policy is *the support of well-being through social action* (ibid.) and the term is used to refer to the way in which governments provide welfare and social protection (Spiker, 2008). Social policy therefore can be seen as the rules, laws and guidelines that organise welfare services, such as education, social services, health, social security, criminal justice service, social work; in fact any body or organisation that aims to support citizens. How services are organised and funded; what services are provided and to whom; who gives the support and how these services are carried out, including the role of the service user, are all governed by social policy (Blakemore, 2003).

Political ideology

Developing social policy is not a politically neutral process (Alcock et al., 2000; Anning et al. 2006, p. 4) but is influenced by and therefore reflects the dominant 'political ideology'. Ideology can be defined as, *any system of ideas underlying and informing social and political action* (Jary and Jary, 2002). Political ideology can therefore be defined more specifically as *a set of related beliefs and values that are organised to form a 'concrete programme of action' to achieve certain social management and organisation*. In other words, people from different political points of view will see different causes or factors as needing attention; more than that, they will have different ideas about how to address these problems and different solutions, which reflect their political view.

Political ideology shapes social policy in a number of ways: first, different political ideologies identify different issues as 'problems to be addressed' and produce different ways of addressing these problems. Second, different political ideologies see the relationship between the individual and the state in different ways, with each having different roles to play. Third, different political ideologies see the interaction between professional groups and the public in different ways.

Therefore, the political ideology of those in power will influence the social policy agenda, the means of implementation and the expectations of professional bodies to enact these policies. Ultimately, then, the changing political aims of those writing and developing policy will impact on the way we interact with other professionals and service users. The experience service users, such as a family, young person or child, might have of accessing and receiving support varies with the aims of social policy and is shaped by the political view of those in government (Blakemore, 2003).

Welfare state

Social provision is made through the welfare state, that is, the institutions that provide support in all areas, such as health, social care, education and youth work. Therefore our third concept is the welfare state. A welfare state is *any form of state in which there has been extensive state legislation leading to the state provision of support and services intended to improve the quality of people's lives* (Jary and Jary, 2001, p. 701). The welfare state in the UK was set up following the Second World War under a raft of legislation that initially addressed the 'five giants' identified by Beverage (1942) of: Want, Disease, Ignorance, Squalor and Idleness (Fraser, 2003, p. 236). To this end, state-run institutions such as social security, health, education, housing and employment services were established to provide support for British citizens. Although the term 'welfare' is not a static or uniform concept that is easily defined (ibid.), it is generally considered to refer to any support service offered to the public, and has expanded to include, for example, social services and the criminal justice system. How these services are provided are subject to social policy and therefore differ with changing political ideology.

Two main political ideologies are evident: the Conservative government (1979–97), whose approach was underpinned by a neo-liberal ideology, and the current New Labour government (1997–present), whose approach is underpinned by Third Way principles. The debate between these two views centres around three related issues: the relationship between the individual and the state and the associated roles of each; how welfare provision should be structured; and how it should be paid for. To illustrate these points more clearly and to provide a background to changes that saw a move away from segregated, agency-determined support provision to the promotion of integrated, client-led services, we will look at the differences in social policy produced by both the Conservative and the current New Labour governments, with a particular focus on the changing role of the individual and professional.

Conservative governments, 1979–97

The Conservative government, led by Margaret Thatcher, took a neo-liberal approach. The central tenets of this political ideology are: individualism and the power of the consumer, the need for the UK to be competitive in the emerging globalised market and the importance of the free market economy in this process. This political philosophy was apparent in their approach to providing welfare services.

The neo-liberal approach promotes the importance of individualism, seeing welfare and other support as the responsibility of the individual and their family. From this perspective, the welfare state providing comprehensive welfare for all was seen as expensive, inefficient and ineffective (Mooney, 2006 and as a source of further problems, such as a 'dependency culture', (see Murray, 1984). The neo-liberal solution to these 'problems of welfare' was to 'roll back' the welfare state and provide, where possible, residual support, with the state providing a 'safety net' in the last resort (George and Miller, 1994), targeted on those most in need. Targeting, they argued, would allow limited resources to help the most vulnerable, increase both efficiency and effectiveness of services and reduce public spending without cutting services.

Second, in order for the UK to be competitive in the emerging global market, it was necessary to develop a national 'flexible workforce', which was both skilled and able to move in and out of work as required by business needs (Jordan, 2006). Previously, large industries offered full-time permanent work and a 'job for life'; now it was necessary to develop new working patterns, flexible to business needs, such as short-term, part-time and contractual employment, and in this way ensure that the nation remained globally competitive. In this climate, it would be necessary for individuals and families to 'take responsibility' for their own support needs; not only for individuals to move to where the work was but also to save and plan for times when they would not be able to provide for themselves through employment (Atkinson and Moon, 1994).

A third, and related, concept was the notion that the introduction of free market competition into public service provision would drive up standards and reduce the cost of welfare to the public (Smart, 2003). The Conservative government criticised welfare and support services provided to the public by LAs as ineffective and inefficient, and LAs for showing little regard for the opinions and needs of those accessing services (Mooney, 2006). In order to drive up standards, competition was introduced in the form of the 'internal market'. Quasi (internal) markets were established, initially within the NHS, but later extended to all areas of social provision (Burden et al., 2000), where private companies competed for contracts to provide public services through the use of Compulsory Competitive Tendering (Mooney, 2006).

The individual is seen as proactive, and this includes the requirement to exercise consumer power, a concept that reflects the neo-liberal notion of 'freedom of choice'. The individual becomes a consumer of welfare services, making 'rational decisions' in the marketplace (Cooper, 2008). If 'choice' is offered, then individuals would be able to 'shop around' between services. This in turn would build competition, especially as it would provide a market between private and state-run provision. For example, in the spheres of health and education, state provision remained, albeit under 'new management', and the opportunities to 'go private' were expanded, increasing levels of competition within the new 'internal economy' of welfare provision (Fraser, 2003). An example of Conservative social policy that reflects neo-liberal political ideology is the Education Reform Act 1988.

Education Reform Act 1988

The changes made to education under this Act parallel the neo-liberal concerns of 'new' management approaches, the use of the internal market and consumer power.

Grant Maintained (GMS) and Locally Managed Schools (LMS) were introduced to take the place of the existing comprehensive school system. These new school structures represented a different approach to management and budgeting. GMSs, those schools who 'opted out' of LEA control, were managed by a governing body that represented teachers, parents and local business, amongst others. They had to manage their own budget and were centrally funded, receiving finances directly from the Department of Education (DoE; DfE), and were entitled to determine their own entry and selection policy (Blakemore, 2003, p. 119). LMSs, those who did not opt out, also were charged with managing a portion of the budget (85 per cent of it; Alcock et al., 2000) and planning development, with LEAs retaining reduced but significant involvement (ibid., p. 181). Specialist schools were established following this reorganisation. These schools were joint funded, part from government and part from business.

Finally, to address issues of control, the Conservative government sought to reduce the power 'socialist' LAs had over the provision of services (Craig, 1989, p. 14). To this end, they devolved power to the institutions themselves, using the business model and 'managerialism' that took methods from the sphere of private business (Mooney, 2006).

The introduction of the National Curriculum aimed to return 'back to basics' and focus on 'core' skills. To provide some uniformity across the education system, the Secretary of State for Education determined what subjects were to be taught, how this was to be carried out, in relation to methods used and when this occurred in relation to the timing in the day, in the term and in the school career of an individual student.

National standards were also set and schools were monitored against these by OfSTED (Office for Standards in Education), a quango responsible for monitoring the quality of education nationally. In addition, new forms of monitoring came into place, such as school league tables and standardised testing (SATS) to provide parents and other concerned 'service users' with a knowledge base from which to make decisions and exercise 'freedom of choice' in relation to schools attended.

All these reforms were brought in with the aim of strengthening the 'voice' of education consumers, such as parents and businesses (Blakemore, 2003, p. 119). The aim of the reorganisation of schools was to decentralise school management away from LEAs to the school itself and to increase standards through competition as funds were allocated on the basis of numbers of students enrolled in a school (Alcock et al., 2000).

An evaluation of Conservative policies

The neo-liberal approach of the Conservative government has been criticised on a number of levels, in relation to their concept of the roles of the individual and state, the movement towards a 'flexible economy', the introduction of the internal market to public service provision, the notion of 'choice' based on consumer power and the associated reduction in locally based power of democratically elected councils.

Incorporating the concepts of individualism and consumerism resulted in disparities being blamed on the individual rather than seen as a result of the unequal social structure (Baumann, 1998). This focus on individual responsibility reflected an increased moral strand (Mooney, 2006), where regulation through the criminal justice system and benefit sanctions were seen as the legitimate response, rather than tackling the structural inequalities (Cooper, 2008, p. 78). An example of this move towards the individual and family as responsible for their own support can be seen in the 1984 Social Security Act, which removed the right of 16–18 year olds to claim benefit entitlements and reduced the rate of benefit for those under 25 years (Alcock et al., 2000), increasing the level of support many young people needed from their families and leaving children at increasing risk of poverty (Cooper, 2008).

The need for a 'flexible workforce' had actually resulted in an increase in social inequality and a growing gap between the rich and the poor (Muschamp and Naidoo, 2002). This had been interpreted by neo-liberals as evidence of an emerging 'underclass' immersed in a 'dependency culture' (Murray, 1984), rather than the impact of structural changes, for example made to the employment structure.

Introducing the internal market into service provision challenged the autonomy of many professional groups (Blakemore, 2003, p. 122), arguably leading to a more fragmented service, focused on budgets rather than the quality of services provided. The neo-liberal approach to the relationship between the individual and the state led to a reduction in the scale and significance of welfare provided by the state and increased and enhanced the role of the private sector in the delivery of services by 'for profit' organisations (Mooney, 2006, p. 256).

Although 'choice' was presented as vital, and exercising that choice as consumer power, access to genuine 'choice' is doubtful (Muschamp and Naidoo, 2002). There was in fact a move from local towards centralised power, and despite apparently increasing 'consumer' control, Conservative policy actually had the effect of limiting the scope of the public sector (Jordan, 2006) and therefore reducing the power of locally elected councils over the provision of local services (Mooney, 2006). The weakening of LAs in turn led to the loss of many public services and welfare entitlements (Hudson, 2002). The remaining state provision was increasingly directed at government programmes which delivered central government agendas and reflected the interests of the business community (Cooper, 2008, p. 75). For example, as a result of the shift in decision making towards individual schools and the seemingly increased service user control and parental 'choice', power had in fact moved from locally elected councils towards centralised power; and institutions were monitored by centralised bodies (such as OfSTED), using standards defined by central government. The National Curriculum emphasised this shift and represented a micro-level control by central government over what went on in classrooms, how and when. In addition, this one-size-fits-all approach marginalised children within diverse communities (Alcock et al., 2000); SATS represented a return to selection (the '11 plus' under another name) and would therefore label children as 'failures' at an early age (ibid.).

This particular notion of 'choice' had its basis in the concept of consumerism rather than democratic accountability. Far from increasing 'choice' of individual citizens, the social policy aims of the Conservative government reflected governance that was 'top down', with little consultation. Second, 'choice' requires access to full information as a basis of decision making; this was not satisfactorily provided. League tables were criticised for their rough measurement, as they did not account for the relative nature of attainment within schools; not all schools started from the same place; and attainment, standards and progress within schools reflect problems in the wider community, such as poverty and the transitory nature of the families of children attending them (Alcock, et al., 2000).

New Labour governments, 1997–

Tony Blair came to power in the 1997 election, bringing with him a new political ideology, a different definition of the 'problems' to be addressed and a different approach to the notion of providing services to the population. The Third Way ethos, theorised by Giddens (1998), sought to combine both sides of the traditional political debate; taking some ideas from neo-liberal ideology and combining these with some notions central to the previous social democratic stance of 'old' Labour. The Blair government focused on the 'modernisation' of welfare provision, engaging in what became known as New Labour's Twenty-First Century Project (Mooney, 2006, p. 256). Modernisation of Public Services (DETR, 1999), states four key principles:

1. A high standard of provision and full accountability.

2. Devolution of decision making about service delivery to the front line to encourage diversity and local innovation and creativity.

3. Flexibility of employment so that staff are better able to deliver modern public services.

4. Promotion of alternative providers (private/voluntary), thus offering greater choice for users.

Underlying this approach are the Third Way principles of equal worth, opportunities for all, the importance of responsibility and the notion of community (Driver and Martell, 2000). Continuities and differences are apparent between the two approaches.

Continuities

New Labour built on Thatcher's reforms (Mooney, 2006, p. 256), discouraging 'welfare dependence' (Cooper, 2008, p. 98). For example, 'welfare to work' schemes such as New Deal saw the individual as responsible for ensuring their own provision of welfare and continued to use the sanctions approach to those claiming benefits who did not take up the support offered by the Job Centre to achieve employment.

New Labour placed a 'communitarian' emphasis on rights and responsibilities, which paralleled the neo-liberal emphasis on 'individualism'. The role of the state was seen as one of 'enabling' rather than 'providing', as it had been under 'old' Labour, leaving responsibility for provision at the door of the individual and family, and ultimately the community (Cooper, 2008, p. 98).

Mooney (2006, p. 255) states that the continuities consisted of choice, competition, the notion of service users as 'customers' and 'consumers', and the concept of performance-related pay, leading to a new 'welfare consensus', with key elements of mixed welfare and an increased provision being made by private business and voluntary groups; a focus on cost control and efficiency, a continuation of the use of 'managerialism' (Mooney, 2006) and a focus on the individual with certain responsibilities (Anning et al., 2006, p. 4).

These similarities are possibly the result of the constraints placed on policy development, such as the legal process of policy-making that all parties must use whilst introducing any new legislation; a balance between economic cost and the amount of public money available; and the level of political acceptability particular policies have and the legacy of previous policy (Blakemore, 2003, p. 114).

Differences

New Labour presented a new 'social contract' between state and individual (Clarke and Newman, 2001), which saw the government's role as being one of 'regulator' and 'enabler', rather than 'provider'. As regulator, the government was responsible for the development of expected standards and monitoring service provision against these. As enabler, the government's role was to provide opportunities for people to equip themselves to be competitive in the global market (France, 2007).

Alongside this development, New Labour rejected the competitive relationship between state and market evident in the neo-liberal free-market approach and instead legislated to support partnership working between all three sectors: business, voluntary and state in the provision of welfare services; with the progress of partnerships being measured against centrally defined performance target indicators (Cooper, 2008).

A third difference was the way in which social problems were defined and understood. New Labour saw social problems as complex and aimed to tackle 'joined up problems with joined up government' (France, 2007, p. 62). Although there are some similarities with the neo-liberal emphasis on 'individualism', New Labour saw structural factors and the inequality of opportunity also as part of the problem. To tackle these issues of inequality, government support agencies, such as the Social Exclusion Unit, were set up to work across departments in order to provide and develop 'joined-up solutions'. New Labour tackled social exclusion using a three-pronged strategy of: 'Getting people to work better', where education and employment training were provided as a right and individuals had the responsibility to access these opportunities and to not get involved in risky behaviour; 'Getting places to work better', that is, developing area-based policy targeting health, education and family services, as well as encouraging community involvement; and finally, 'service providers to perform better' and provide 'joined-up thinking, co-ordination and integration of service provision' (Cooper, 2008, p. 41).

New Labour aimed to tackle social exclusion at a neighbourhood level. For example, in their first term in office they established a range of schemes, such as Education Action Zones, Health Action Zones, New Deal for Communities, Sure Start, Excellence in Cities and Employment Action Zones. These schemes aimed to put residents at the heart of decision making in relation to services and provision within their own communities (ibid., p. 143).

Where the main neo-liberal focus had been on the individual and family, with the notion that 'there is no such thing as society' (Thatcher, 1984), New Labour aimed, through the concept of 'communitarianism', to build communities of hard-working, law-abiding responsibilised citizens, who govern themselves (Cooper, 2008). 'Communitarianism' can be defined as:

> *a discourse that emphasises the need for the state to generate social interaction between individuals 'in community' in order to strengthen civic society and, thereby, community safety, cohesion and well-being.*

(ibid., pp. 127–128)

To pull these ideas together and provide a basis from which to identify the implications of this policy approach on inter-agency working, professional practice and the experience of the service user, we will look more closely at the policy background as developed and implemented by New Labour in relation to employment and social exclusion; education and employability; and policy specifically aimed to support children and their families.

Employment policy and social exclusion

Under the 'new social contract' of rights and responsibilities, New Labour replaced the idea that the state was responsible to ensure full youth employment with the concept of 'employability' (Blakemore, 2003). Employability refers to the level of education, training, experience and appropriate attitude of each working-aged person, as well as expressing the opportunities available to them to access jobs, and represents their chances of gaining employment in the work marketplace. The New Labour interpretation is that, to reduce social exclusion, an individual must be in employment, therefore one approach to reducing social exclusion is to increase individual 'employability' (France, 2007) and increase the employment options available to them. Education and training is the best way to achieve this and is therefore a way to reduce social exclusion (Social Exclusion Unit, 2006).

To address these issues, New Deal, introduced in 1997 was aimed at 16–18 year olds (Mizen, 2004) and included many of the sanctions put in place by the previous Conservative government, linking benefits to work and requiring job seekers to fulfil certain criteria, such as providing proof of job searching, attending a 'work-focused interview' with a personal advisor at the Job Centre and maintaining a presentable appearance; in addition, imposing penalties for not fulfilling these requirements (Finn, 2003). In addition, Connexions was established in 2002, to provide all 13–19 year olds with a personal adviser (PA), to be 'powerful friends' (Coles et al., 2004) and act as advocates for young people by liaising with local services, such as education, training, benefits, health, housing, and support groups (anger management, drug rehabilitation).

The New Deal sanctions, however, were criticised for causing more problems than they solved. For example, they led to the problem of 'disappearing' youth, as young people were removed from the official statistics, and increased youth cynicism in relation to employment; ultimately they affected the most vulnerable (France, 2007).

The focus on the individual exposes an underlying philosophy that sees problems as arising as a result of young people's individual failings (Mizen, 2004); victim-blaming ignores the impact of structural inequality in the distribution of resources and money (Byrne, 2006). Instead, there is an increased focus on poor parenting, the influence of a disruptive peer group culture and an individual lack of interest in schools (MacDonald and March, 2005).

The concept of 'employability' has also been criticised, as it gives market forces a major role in setting youth employment levels and wages and again relates youth unemployment to individual deficiencies and failings (France, 2007). In addition, it is not clear that this approach is successful, as 'learning targets' for 19–21 year olds were missed (DfES, 2004), high rates of truancy, permanent exclusions and illiteracy on leaving school continued and a 9 per cent increase in the number of NEETS between 1999 and 2004 occurred (SEU, 2006).

Education and employability

When New Labour came to power, education was identified as a key policy (Blakemore, 2003, p. 116), seeing it as a neglected service, with poor standards. Parents were concerned that 'choices' they had been given by the Conservative government had not resulted in an increased access to true decision making but a shortage of places in desirable schools and increased divisions between schools in different areas (France, 2007). Teaching as a profession was framed as being 'in crisis' (Anning et al., 2006).

To improve teaching standards, the Schools Standards and Framework Act 1998 was introduced, giving the government new powers to tackle failing schools through naming and shaming of failed LEAs and, on some occasions, passing governance to private companies.

To increase educational attainment in areas of social exclusion and poverty, Education Action Zones were established as schools in poorer areas grouped together. The government also provided funding to encourage partnerships between local businesses, schools and LEAs, aiming to develop innovative ways of linking education and employment. In addition, Specialist Schools were developed, leading to an increase of religious-based schools, a decrease in comprehensive schools and an emergence of New City Academies, where the private sector (business) were dominant in governance.

New Labour, therefore, kept neo-liberal notions of competition and consumerist power (Blakemore, 2003), maintaining the internal market and micro-management of schools through the National Curriculum, standardised testing (SATs) and centralised control through inspection by OfSTED. However, they extended this, introducing Daily Literacy Hour in primary schools, an approach which parallels the Conservative 'back to basics' policy and represents an increase in central control.

Education provided for children with special educational needs was also reviewed. Excellence For All Children: Meeting Special Educational Needs (DfES, 1998) stated that agencies should work together to provide responsive support to vulnerable children, children with special needs and their families (Anning et al., 2006). The subsequent Special Educational Needs Code of Practice (2001) allowed for early identification and diagnosis of problems and emphasised the importance of multidisciplinary working.

A further addition to this approach was the notion of Lifelong Learning (France 2007), with three core beliefs: the need to develop human capital to meet the competition needs of employers and the economy; individuals have a responsibility to invest in themselves; individuals have a responsibility to increase and manage their own employability. This need for skilling and education goes beyond school years and is a constant element throughout an individual's career. This approach reflects links New Labour makes between individual responsibility and the need for the nation to be competitive in the global market.

Central to New Labour's approach, and reflecting their emphasis on the proactive citizen, is a focus on 'citizenship'. This has been introduced to the national curriculum and aims to address the perceived problem of political apathy amongst young people.

Children and family services

New Labour policy emphasises the importance of inter-agency collaboration in the development of children's services (Anning et al., 2006). For example, the National Service Framework for Children, Young People and Maternity Services (DfES and DoH, 2004) represents a plan of action that requires all agencies to work in a holistic, 'joined-up' way. To address the issue of social exclusion, policies such as the Children's Fund (established 2000) and Sure Start (1998) were implemented, aiming to provide prevention services that would meet the needs of vulnerable 5–11 year olds in 149 English LAs through collaborative team working (Anning et al., 2006).

Following the Climbié case, the Laming Report (2003) highlighted problems in child protection, such as the problem of individual cases 'falling through the net'. As a result, the green paper Every Child Matters (DfES, 2003) was put out for consultation amongst both specialists and the public; and gave rise to the policy document Every Child Matters: Change for Children (DfES, 2004), the Children Act 2004 and subsequent Youth Matters (2005b), aimed at young adults and teenagers. This raft of legislation required LAs to appoint an officer to coordinate local children and family services and develop a Children and Young People's Plan (by 2006). The Children's Trust was set up, with a responsibility to make arrangements for allocating funds to children's services.

Children's Centres were established, initially in areas of greater social exclusion and later expanded cross-nationally, to act as sites for integrated delivery of services to under school-aged children and their families. For school-aged children and their families, extended schools, both mainstream and special, were seen as a 'hub' for service provision, providing 'wrap around care' before and after school, sporting and out of school opportunities, as well as parenting support, specialist support (such as therapy and behaviour support) and family learning opportunities (Anning et al., 2006).

ACTIVITY *1.1*

- *How are the concepts of political ideology and social policy linked?*

- *Can you give examples of two different approaches to the relationship between the individual and the state and the political ideology that shapes each?*

The implications of the current social policy context on practice

Effective communication is necessary to ensure good service provision on three levels, between agencies, between professionals and between the individual seeking support and those that provide it (Kennedy Report, 2001).

Inter-agency working

Inter-agency working is required for the provision of 'joined-up' services (Leathard, 2003) and refers to how different providers, for example the state, private or voluntary sectors, of a range of services should work together to provide a 'seamless service' (DoH, 2000). New Labour policies reflect the aims of multi-agency working (Anning et al., 2006), for example multi-agency working is specified in *Every Child Matters* (DfES, 2004a) and *Youth Matters* (DfES, 2005) as part of the strategy to achieve the stated aims (Frost, 2005, p. 13).

Key factors needed for successful multi-agency working include clear leadership and a clear focus, with common aims and knowledge of other professional roles and working activities. This approach requires commitment, regular meetings and time spent by professionals to learn the necessary communication skills (Atkinson et al., 2001). More specifically, it requires shared information systems and assessment frameworks (Common Assessment Framework, 2004) and, at an extreme, joint planning, funding and intervention strategies (Anning et al., 2006, pp. 5–6). To avoid conflict, Frost (2005) suggests inter-agency working must be based on formal structures to guide liaison with other agencies and agree how team members are to be managed. Clarity is also necessary in relation to team aims and objectives.

Inter- and intra-professional collaboration

Policy encourages interprofessional collaboration in its aim to provide holistic services. This also reflects the aim of moving from a one-size-fits-all approach, where agency concerns are central and provision is structured in relation to requirements of professional or political bodies. Rather than individuals fitting in with the types of education, health care and family services available, professionals are required to consider the needs of the individual. To accomplish this, the concept of inter-professional collaboration is used; it refers to the desire to structure professional working that puts individuals and their self-defined needs at the centre of agency response. This approach cuts down on repetition, intrusion and the possibility of competing solutions, and aims to maximise the professional skills to address individual issues, to provide 'bespoke' support (hopefully with a better chance of success). To achieve this personalisation, accurate and appropriate communication is needed on two levels: first, intra-professional communication, which refers to communication between workers in the same profession; second, inter-professional communication, which refers to communication between workers of different professions to provide a coordinated response (Leathard, 2003).

Inter-/intra-professional collaboration is marked by a shared vision of teamwork and a shared philosophy of support provision (Vanclay, 2003, p. 169); all team members are expected to contribute to problem-solving and decision making and share responsibilities for team actions. Central to the success of this approach is effective communication, in relation to information and knowledge-sharing and an appreciation of differing professional concerns (ibid.). In addition, a clear understanding of roles and boundaries is necessary to avoid confusion and conflicts and to ensure a holistic approach. Skills should ideally be pooled and all professionals in the team should have the opportunity to learn new skills in a team environment (Miller and Freeman, 2003, p. 123) and take part in inter-professional learning.

The use of this approach has certain implications for professional practice. First, active sharing of information is essential; however, it must be acknowledged that this requires mutual trust and reflects a tension between a need to share information and a need to maintain confidentiality (DPA, 1998; Vanclay, 2003, p. 169). Second, this represents a type of working that requires both patience and time in order to develop and maintain interpersonal relationships. Third, this type of working represents a change in the role of the professional as it requires an advocatory element; the professional mediates and negotiates between the services available and the needs of the individual (Engel and Gursky, 2003, p. 48).

Inter-/intra-professional collaboration has a number of advantages. It is client-centred, reducing the impact of agency agendas and professional interests and supporting individual choice and rights. It is holistic, as it allows for a joined-up approach. It is effective, as it leads to solutions tailor-made to individual needs and is therefore more likely to work. It is efficient, as it reduces the overlap of professional roles and repetitions (for example, in assessment). Finally, it allows for a positive work experience and skills building (Leathard, 2003).

A range of barriers that work against inter-/intra-professional collaboration has been identified. Although policy has considered joint-working between professionals as of central importance in the assessment and action planning required to provide child protection and family support since the 1970s (DHSS, 1974, 1976, 1980; Parton, 1985), some have identified practical problems related to implementing policy effectively in practice and problems associated with realistic planning (Farmer, 1999). Professional cultural differences (Ouvretveit, 1990), such as different 'languages' and values (Pietroni, 1992), and conflicting professional and organisational boundaries and loyalties can complicate communication. This is compounded by different professional groups receiving separate training and workers having different training backgrounds; for example, some are professionally trained and some are considered non-professional (Hudson, 2002). Status differences are further emphasised by inequalities in pay. There are certain practical barriers. This approach to professional working relies on a clear definition of roles; however, this is not always possible in practice – different leadership styles apparent within different professional groups and the need for regular meetings can contribute to poor communication (ibid.). It is important to acknowledge and address these barriers; however, this requires commitment from key managers and budget-holders (Rummery and Glendinning, 2000).

ACTIVITY *1.2*

Identify the factors that facilitate inter-professional working and those barriers that restrict this type of professional interaction.

Client empowerment

Central to the notion of collaborative inter-professional working is changing the need relationship between the professional and the individual service user and, as a result, a changing approach to the role of the individual. Neo-liberal approaches saw the individual as a 'consumer' of support provision, with access to certain choices about the services and the support they consume. New Labour built on this approach, seeing the role of the individual as central, with the leading voice in participation and decision making, and the professional role as one of advocate, guide and advisor. Therefore, individuals are seen as proactive consumers of support, with a role that places them central to the team at one extreme or as part of the team at another.

The personalisation of support results when the individual is able to exercise their autonomy, have a say and have this view 'heard' (Roberts, 2002). In order to have a say in what happens to their individual cases, however, full information must be provided as it underpins informed decision making necessary in law (Butler, 2002). Where people are not able to make decisions, the professional role is to support them in identifying particular needs and helping them to express these so that the individual view can take centre stage in decision making.

Evidently this is skilled work as it requires the building of empathetic, trusting and respectful relationships, as well as an understanding on the part of the professional that their role is that of advisor and advocate, aiming to identify service users' needs as they see them and use this view as the starting point for further planning and structuring of support provision.

Within this model, the service user view is central to planning and structuring of support provision. Service users should be in the driving seat, where possible, making decisions relating to their own support; where barriers to this process exist, professionals should be identifying and action planning in order that service users have the support they need to explore their situation and the potential options available to meet those needs.

This is more than just 'letting service users decide'; it is about empowering action by professionals to ensure all necessary information is provided, that options and potential outcomes are fully explored, so that people are making decisions about their support with an understanding of the implications and supported in this 'work' by professionals.

It is this interaction between professionals and services users – involving managing an empowering and respectful relationship, containing aspects of advocate, advisor, counsellor and friend – that enables service users to truly take their part in the inter-collaborative team aiming to meet their needs, as the individual sees them, with personalised, joined-up services. This complex and dynamic relationship, where power is shared (or, at an extreme, lies in the hands of service users) and support is structured in relation to individually self-defined needs, is a far cry from those relationships between professionals and the public, where the professional 'knows best' and dictates the plan of action based on professionally defined priorities and structured by agency agendas – a move from 'doing to' to 'being with' (McCormack, 2001) service users. In this way, the most appropriate and therefore potentially the most successful support arrangements can be made.

ACTIVITY **1.3**

With their training background and expert knowledge, professionals are in a better position than service users to make decisions about the support an individual needs. Discuss.

C H A P T E R S U M M A R Y

There are a number of central strands in this debate. The aims of social policy, and the means to achieve those ends, have altered with changing dominant political ideology; that is, how the relationship between state and individual is conceived and the issues that are defined as problems; how the debate in relation to the distribution of resources is managed, in relation to the wider socio-economic environment and across services and between individuals

This is evident in the changing emphasis on policy that has changed from a context of service provision that is agency- and professional-led, where the interests and concerns of both agency and professional are central drivers in decision making at three levels: *micro* – professional with a paternalistic role, with control and power within action planning and the implementation of this plan when working with individuals; *meso* – separate working, where individual cases were managed by distinct professional groups, working within separate locations and working within different professional cultural enclaves; and *macro* – where policy was decided by powerful 'others' and services that were made available were decided with professional, but little service user, consultation.

Effective communication ensures that those at the centre of decision making, the service users themselves, have access to the full information they need to make decisions and are able to discuss and negotiate those decisions and to have the action plan devised for implementing those decisions explained in a way they can understand. Communication is not just important; it is integral to the assessment of needs and implementation of support provision. Effective communication is a skill that is central to any work that aims to support people.

FURTHER READING

Sutton, CD (2006) *Helping families with troubled children: A preventive approach*. Chichester and Hoboken, NJ: Wiley.

This book provides a number of ways of working with children and their families that supports proactive participation between service user and professionals and provides some guidance and creative ideas in relation to how to implement empowering professional practice.

Sayer, T (2008) *Critical practice in working with children*. Basingstoke: Palgrave Macmillan.

This book provides further information and analysis of the policy context within which social workers practise to produce joined-up, personalised services.

Chapter 2

What is communication? The process of transferring information

Ally Dunhill

Objectives

By the end of this chapter, you should have an understanding of:

- Integrated practices of communicating and engaging with children, young people, parents, carers and other professionals.

- Theories and skills of engagement in communication.

- Miscommunication and the problems that can occur.

- The developmental process of communication and how it transforms and transmits to all areas of life: the home environment, at school, within the community, at work and within work and beyond.

- The opportunities in which children, young people and adults transfer information to professionals.

- The significant change effective communication can bring to relationships with children, young people, families, carers and other professionals.

Introduction

Communication is a 'two-way' process, with a very broad theoretical base. It is an area of study that has supported a range of research identifying many levels and complexities. Communication has been described as both a simple and complex process (Rosengren, 2000). Communication is a skill that is not always simple and straightforward to learn and develop. To be able to communicate effectively can require a great deal of practice and dedication.

Integrated working provides a 'one stop shop' for children, young people, families and carers, where they can access a range of services, all located under one roof or very close together. These services include 'everyone who works with children and young people, part or all of the time' (CWDC, 2008, p. 2). When working within integrated services, effective communication and engagement with children, young people, families, carers and other professionals is essential to ensure that integrated support is identified, planned and provided.

Children, young people and families will come into contact with a wide range of individuals who are commonly called professionals. These individuals include social workers, personal advisers, youth workers, family workers, health visitors, midwives, community children's nurses, school nurses, substance misuse workers, nursery nurses, educational welfare officers, teachers, and support staff such as learning mentors working in schools. These professionals can work within voluntary sector organisations or statutory services (DfES, 2005b). Professionals working within integrated services can bring different values, beliefs and qualities gained from the training and experiences each person has experienced and received. This can lead to differences in what support needs different professionals identify and offer (Glenny and Roaf, 2008).

The Laming (2003) report into the death of eight-year-old Victoria Climbié clearly stated that, although children and young people were identified as requiring support and intervention and had contact with a number of agencies, it was still possible for them to fall through the net. The government's response was the Every Child Matters (ECM) Green Paper (2003) and the Children Act 2004.The Children Act 2004 led to a number of organisational changes in children's services, including appointing a director within local authorities and creating Children's Trusts and Local Safeguarding Children Boards, which was the starting point in providing an integrated service for children and young people.

When working with children, young people, families and carers, a professional's role will not only involve communication, but actually relies on it. The number of agencies that support children and young people has grown, while the issues children and young people are experiencing have widened and became more complex. Communicating effectively across these agencies has become essential to identifying the needs and planning the support for each child or young person. Communication forms a large proportion of the work undertaken by professionals in the children's workforce and is the ingredient that brings all of the agencies together, ensures they become 'joined up' and allows integrated working to be carried out. To be able to become 'joined up', professionals need an awareness of other professionals and agencies and knowledge of their roles and responsibilities. As stated in the Common Core of Skills and Knowledge: Multi-agency Working, professionals should:

> *Have a general knowledge and understanding of the range of organisations and individuals working with children, young people and those caring for them, and be aware of the roles and responsibilities of other professionals.*
>
> (DfES, 2005, p. 19)

Communication is arguably the most important skill that is required by professionals in organisations.

When a child, young person or adult communicates at any time they perceive the other person's responses and react with their own previous knowledge and experience. Inevitably they are not always recognising the multi-levels and complexity of the interaction that they are engaging in. It is only by paying attention during the interaction with a child, young person or adult that the professional will have any idea about what to say or do next to ensure they communicate effectively; this is sometimes easier said than done. Effective engagement in communicating with children, young people, adults, families and carers needs to be clear and at the level required for the receiver to understand without being condescending. As Marsen (2006, p. 32) states:

> *Miscommunication occurs when the message does not reach the receiver in the way it was intended by the sender.*

To ensure that miscommunication does not occur, written and spoken exchanges need to be expressed in straightforward language, avoiding jargon. In many agencies and work environments a wide array of abbreviations, phrases and key words are used, many of which may be associated with a particular profession, region or even team, and much of this professional language includes terms not used in a home environment. When communicating with children, young people or families and carers this can cause communication problems, confusion and raise concerns among everyone.

Miscommunication is a common problem and can cause frustration and even conflict between the sender and receiver. This has major implications not only for the professional but impacts on the service and support provided for the children, young people, adults, families and carers. For example, different agencies or working environments have different titles for staff doing the same or a similar role. Schools employ teaching assistants (TAs), classroom assistants (CAs), learning support assistants (LSAs), child support assistants (CSAs) or special needs assistants (SNAs). If any of these abbreviations or terms are used during meetings or in any form of communication and are not recognised by all the attendees or receivers, then a miscommunication can occur. Professionals should, 'appreciate that others may not have the same understanding of professional terms and may interpret abbreviations such as acronyms differently' (DfES, 2005, p. 18).

> *Good communication is central to working with children, young people, their families and carers. It is a fundamental part of the Common Core. It involves listening, questioning, understanding and responding to what is being communicated by children, young people and those caring for them.*
>
> (ibid., p. 6)

The term 'communication' covers just about any interaction with another person. It includes conveying, sharing, exchanging, transmitting, broadcasting and receiving information, ideas and feelings between people. In its simplest form, communication can be defined as the process of transmitting information from one person to another.

Involvement in communication

Effective communication and engagement requires the involvement of children, young people, parents, carers and professionals, from the start. This should begin with ensuring that everyone is involved, and consulted with, in the design and delivery of services and decisions that affect them in a format that they understand and can access. Effective communication only occurs when the meaning of a message is received as the sender intended it to be.

The government's model for integrating services for children and young people utilises the current networks of relationships and resources within the current children's workforce. This is achieved through creating a flexible workforce, which includes new agencies, with a wide range of transferrable skills and expertise. These include communication skills, shared knowledge of roles, responsibilities, standards and benchmarks.

Effective communication is a two-way process and most children, young people, parents and carers can recognise when professionals are genuinely interested in them. It follows that only when everyone is comfortable with the process will two-way communication and engagement happen and truly be effective. A key part of effective communication and engagement is trust, both between the professionals, children, young people, parents and their carers, and within the different sectors of the workforce itself. It is crucial that professionals consult with children, young people, parents and carers and consider their opinions and perspectives from the outset in an open and honest manner. This ensures the views, opinions and experiences of everyone will be heard and should then be taken into account.

There has been a wide range of global, national and local initiatives, and policy and legislative developments to involve children, young people, adults and families in actively participating and engaging in consultations. These generally apply to all children and young people aged from 0 to 19 years.

These include:

- UN Convention of the Rights of the Child (1989).

- Health and Social Care Act (2001).

- Every Child Matters (2003).

- Children Act (2004).

- Youth Matters (2005).

- Childcare Act (2006).

- Early Years Foundation Stage (2008).

- National Service Framework for children, young people and maternity services.

- 10 Year Childcare Strategy.

- Joint Area Reviews.

- Participation Strategy for Children and Young People.

Examples of legislation to support participation are:

- *Every Child Matters* (DfES, 2003), which aims to ensure that we take into account the direct views of children and young people, who are not automatically consulted, in addition to the perspectives of parents, professionals and other significant adults in order to provide effective services designed around their needs.

- *The Early Years Foundation Stage* (DCSF, 2008a), which makes reference to the requirement to listen to young children, parents and carers.

- *Section 3(5) of the Childcare Act* (2006), which places a duty on local authorities in England to have regard for the views of young children from birth to five when providing early childhood services. This also meets the requirements under Article 12 of the UN Convention on the Rights of the Child, which was adopted by the United Nations in 1989 and ratified by the UK in 1991 (Lancaster, 2006).

- *Article 12 (Respect for the views of the child)*, which states: 'When adults are making decisions that affect children, children have the right to say what they think should happen and have their opinions taken into account' (United Nations Convention on the Rights of the Child, 1989).

This list is not exhaustive; it is representative of the wide range of opportunities that children, young people, adults and families had or have to actively participate and engage in consultations. Children and young people's views are increasingly sought by a range of organisations and individuals. Collecting children and young people's thoughts and ideas and involving them in the decision-making process are part of policy and practice procedures relating to working within this sector (Crow et al., 2008). Consultation with children and young people should be normal practice in the process that affects them directly or indirectly and should be carried out not because it is seen as good practice or because of policy, but because children and young people have a right to be heard.

Communication skills

Communication skills are often classified as verbal or non-verbal. Communication skills, perhaps not surprisingly, feature highly in the list of skills that professionals consider important for integrated services when working with children, young people, parents and carers. Communication skills such as listening, questioning and paraphrasing alongside understanding, recognising and using body language are essential for professionals to develop a trusting relationship with children, young people, parents and carers. This relationship is often referred to as having a rapport.

The way communication is sent and received is equally important. Much communication in today's society is carried out through electronic means but not everyone can access this and some people prefer not to use it. Many people still prefer to receive a letter rather than information over the telephone or by email. The way information is communicated within and between agencies is often governed by how the agencies are structured but it is important that agencies identify and communicate with children, young people, parents and carers using the method that they prefer.

The importance of keeping different lines of communication open and continually providing the opportunity for dialogue between children, young people, parents, carers, professionals and between agencies is paramount. Alongside this, the need for everyone to be willing to discuss issues with others and for them to be open and honest should also be a priority. This does not always happen.

Keeping lines of communication open and engaging with children, young people, parents, carers and other professionals is critical. This, however, may be affected by the past experiences of those people involved in the engagement. Children, young people, parents, carers and professionals may have had negative experiences of communicating in a home environment, at school, within the community or at work. Assumptions are made and misunderstandings occur; these assumptions can then be transformed and transmitted to all areas of life – the home environment, at school, within the community, at work and within work and beyond – resulting in a negative influence on all those involved and influencing all future interactions. For the professional, this means it can influence the way in which participants may behave and respond. This previous negative experience may create some sense of meaning that links previous negative emotions to communicating with a particular professional, agency or group of agencies, resulting in a negative effect on any future communications and interactions.

There are many studies of communication and from these a wide range of definitions, fields and models have been identified. Two major fields of communication studies identified by Marsen (2006) that professionals should be aware of are interpersonal communication and intercultural communication. These areas are defined and dependent on the contexts and the individuals involved.

According to Marsen, interpersonal communication is defined as an interaction between two or more people and can be performed through a range of forms including face to face meetings and emails. Professionals acting as a sender or receiver should be professional at all times. They should ensure they do not make assumptions about the child, young person or adult during any interpersonal interaction as misunderstandings can occur and have a negative effect on the outcome. For example, during a family group conference (where staff from a range of agencies discuss with the family the information about services, resources and support that may be available for a child or young person), one of the agencies represented used abbreviations and terms that caused confusion among the other agencies and the family. This professional had assumed that everyone attending would be aware of the terms that they used regularly within their normal working environment and misunderstandings occurred.

Professionals must also be aware of issues around intercultural communication. This relates to different ethnic groups, practices, values, beliefs and languages. Problems can occur through translations leading to limited understandings or total misunderstanding. Different cultures have different ways of communicating respect and politeness. Expressions, dress codes and non-verbal behaviour can be acceptable in one culture but can sometimes be insulting in another; for example, proximity and eye contact have different meanings for different cultures (ibid.). When communicating, professionals should always be aware of differences in cultures, ethnicity and social groups, be respectful and act without prejudice:

> *Communication is not just about the words you use, but also your manner of speaking, body language and, above all, the effectiveness with which you listen. To communicate effectively it is important to take account of culture and context . . .*
>
> (DfES, 2005, p. 6)

To support an understanding of different cultures, professionals should attend any training opportunities regarding multicultural awareness. Professionals benefit from training within a multi-agency context that includes professionals from a range of agencies and offers opportunities to engage with a range of expertise from all sectors to develop their knowledge and communication skills. Joint training would support and promote 'interaction between the parties to achieve a common goal' (Meads and Ashcroft, 2005, p. 16). Such dialogue would also facilitate a better understanding of how other agencies function and thereby resolve many of the day-to-day issues that arise when working in a multi-agency environment delivering integrated support. Lord Laming (2003) clearly stated the need for professionals working in different agencies to ignore their traditional working boundaries and work together to provide an effective service to children and young people. Professionals who are willing to share and learn will find working within integrated services a highly positive experience.

Dissemination of information

The dissemination of information and the need to give everyone, within a team, individuals and families, feedback on a regular basis and to keep everyone *up to speed* is equally important. This can be difficult when a range of individuals and agencies are involved. For children, young people, parents and carers, having a named person to contact within an agency and being able to put a face to a name are factors that can facilitate effective communication and engagement. In addition, there is a need to share data more effectively to avoid the replication of services or repeat requests for data from key individuals. Using the Common Assessment Framework (CAF) to gather information about a child or young person eliminates repetition. A checklist is completed beforehand to assess whether a CAF is required as it is not required for every child or young person. By completing a CAF, professionals gain early identification of children and young people's needs (Fitzgerald and Kay, 2008). A lead professional will then be appointed to coordinate the required provision and act as a single point of contact for a child and their family when a range of agencies are involved. The lead is usually decided upon at a multi-agency meeting. This and other processes of information sharing must use a common language. This is essential when working with children, young people, families, carers and other professionals to ensure everyone involved understands what is happening around them and what their responsibilities are.

Listening skills

As stated at the start of this chapter, communication is a two-way process. Professionals not only have to effectively send a message but, equally importantly, they have to effectively receive the message. Research states that 55 per cent of communication is non-verbal; only 7 per cent is verbal (words only) and 38 per cent is vocal (including tone of voice, inflection and other sounds) (Mehrabian, 1971). This suggests that, not only are the visual expressions of body language, e.g. gestures and eye contact important, but listening and honing in to the verbal and vocal expressions, e.g. pitch and pace, are key for professionals to fully receive the message from the child, young person or adult.

Listening to children, young people, parents and carers is a necessary requirement to understand what they are feeling and what it is they need. Professionals are required to actively listen and, although it is one of the most important of the non-verbal communication skills, it is often underestimated. It involves hearing, interpreting and constructing meanings and is not just confined to the spoken word, but includes the involvement of all the senses and emotions.

Actively listening to children, young people, parents, carers and other professionals requires professional values of respect and a belief that everyone is worth listening to. Actively listening to children, young people, parents and carers using a range of methods requires the professional to be organised. This includes identifying the methods of communication that the child, young person or adult prefers and ensures that the most appropriate method is used. For example, if a local authority wants to engage with young people to find out their views on the recreation facilities in the area, arranging a face to face meeting may not be the best way to attract a large number of responses. The local authority could send out information through school email addresses and advertise the consultation process on posters and on local radio stations. Although these methods may be more expensive, the number of young people engaging in the consultation process will be greater and a wider range of young people will be consulted with and so the findings of consultation will be gained from a wider representation of young people.

Using a range of methods to gather the views from everyone involved can empower children, young people, parents and carers, allowing them to express their views and opinions and take part in decision making. Sometimes when agencies are involved, children and young people, parents and carers can feel disempowered or removed from the decision-making process. All participants should be seen as key individuals who can inform and enhance the process. Parents and carers have a greater understanding of their children; this includes knowledge of present and previous experiences. The information they provide is vital and ensures that all aspects of the child or young person's life are captured and their needs identified, planned for and supported.

Actively involving children, young people, parents and carers in consultation activities as a strategy for empowerment including decision making and service delivery has the potential to improve many children and young people's lives. Children, young people, parents and carers can also gain new skills and knowledge from such a process (Tucker, 2001).

ACTIVITY 2.1

How do you show you are a good listener?

- *Watch a chat show on the TV. Have a pen and note pad at hand.*

- *List the things the host does to indicate they are paying attention to their guests.*

- *Think about interactions you have had with three people in the last 24 hours. Write down all the non-verbal signals you sent to the receiver during the interaction, e.g. smiles, nods of the head, facial expressions and what you stopped doing or carried on with while they were talking.*

Reflect on these signals and think about:

- *Were they appropriate for the receiver (age appropriate/clear language used)?*

- *How effective were you in demonstrating that you were, or were not, listening?*

- *How do you know you were effective?*

Comment

It can be easier to identify other people's communication skills rather than our own. Try asking those around you if they believe you are an effective listener, why they believe this and what signals you give out when listening.

Developing communication knowledge and skills

Communication skills are complex and draw on a wide range of knowledge and skills (Crow et al., 2008) to be learned and developed. To support this process it is good practice to build a rapport with children, young people, parents, carers and other professionals. Key components of effective communication are respect, trust and honesty, both between the workforce, children, young people, parents and carers, but also between the different agencies within the workforce itself (DfES, 2005b).

The following list of skills and knowledge are a revised version of the original text that appeared in the DfES Common Core of Skills and Knowledge (2005b). They are skills that are required by professionals working within integrated services. They may need to be developed through training, learning or experience but are crucial to ensure professionals can effectively communicate and engage with children, young people, parents, carers and professionals from other agencies and develop a positive working relationship.

Skills

The following skills are necessary for effective communication.

Listening and building empathy
- Establish rapport and respectful, trusting relationships with children, young people, their families, carers and other agencies.

- Develop and use effective communication systems appropriate to the designated audience.

- Communicate effectively with all children, young people, families, carers and other agencies.

- Be aware that some children and young people do not communicate verbally and that you need to adapt your style of communication to their needs and abilities.

- Understand the effects of non-verbal communication such as body language, and appreciate that different cultures use and interpret body language in different ways.

- Build rapport and develop relationships using the appropriate form of communication for your designated audience (for example, spoken language, play, body and sign language).

- Build open and honest relationships by respecting children, young people, parents, carers and professionals from other agencies, making them feel valued as partners.

- Hold conversations at the appropriate time and place, understanding the value of day-to-day contact.

- Actively listen in a calm, open, non-threatening manner and use questions to check understanding and acknowledge that you have heard what is being said.

- Understand the role and value of families and carers as partners in supporting their children to achieve positive outcomes.

Summarising and explaining

- Summarise situations in the appropriate way for the individual you are communicating with (taking into account factors such as background, age and personality).

- Understand how to present genuine choices to children and young people and how to obtain consent to sharing information.

- Explain to the child, young person, parent or carer what kind of information you may have to share with others.

- Explain what has happened or will happen next and check their understanding and, where appropriate, their consent to the process.

Consultation and negotiation

- Consult with the child, young person, parent or carer from the beginning of the process.

- Inform, involve and help the child or young person to assess different courses of action, understand the consequences of each and, where appropriate, agree next steps.

- Understand the key role and value of parents and carers; know when and where to refer them for further sources of information, advice or support.

- Identify what each party hopes to achieve in order to reach the best possible and fair conclusion for the child or young person.

- Share reasons for actions with the child or young person, parent and carer.

- Provide support and encouragement to children and young people.

- Know when and how to hand over control of a situation to others.

Knowledge

The following areas of knowledge are crucial to communication.

How communication works

- Know that communication is a two-way process.

- Know how to listen to children, young people and adults, make them feel valued and involved, and know when it is important to focus on the individual rather than the group.

- Be aware of different ways of communicating, including electronic channels, and understand barriers to communication.

- Be aware that the child, young person, parent or carer may not have understood what is being communicated.

- Know how to report and record information formally and informally in the appropriate way for the audience concerned, including how the use of the Common Assessment Framework for Children and Young People (CAF) helps communication between professionals.

Confidentiality and ethics
- Remember and understand the procedures and legislation relating to confidentiality issues that apply to your job role.

- Understand the limits of confidentiality that apply to your job role and that sometimes it is necessary to go against a child or young person's expressed wishes in their best interests and, where this is the case, ensure that the child or young person understands what is happening and why.

Sources of support
- Know where education and support services for children, young people, parents and carers are available locally.

- Know when and how to refer to sources of information, advice or support from different agencies or professionals.

Importance of respect
- Be self-aware: know how to demonstrate a commitment to treating all children, young people and adults fairly; be respectful by using active listening and avoiding assumptions (DfES, 2005).

ACTIVITY **2.2**

Using the DfES's Common Core of Skills and Knowledge (2005b) as a checklist, score yourself from 5 (being the highest) to 1 (the lowest) against each criteria.

- *Which areas are your strengths and which areas do you need to develop further?*

- *Who or where would you go to for further training to develop these?*

Comment

The above range of knowledge and skills will be explored further throughout this book.

The significant change effective communication can bring to relationships with children, young people, parents and carers
Only when effective communication and engagement takes place and professionals gain a wide range of relevant information can support needs be identified and planned for. When communicating with children, young people, parents and carers it can be beneficial to the

process if the professional engages with the child, young person or adult holistically. This can be as simple as starting conversations around what the child, young person or adult is interested in to start the communication and engagement process. For example, during a home visit, the young person involved looks rather nervous and has made little or no eye contact when the professional arrives. The young person is wearing a particular football shirt. The professionals starts the conversation around that team, their favourite team or sport in general. The young person then may want to talk about a range of information about their team, where it is in the league, how it is being managed. This can make the young person feel less nervous and once a rapport has been created the young person may be more receptive to questions and engage in the discussion about themself.

Time will be required to allow the child or young person to express themself, both emotionally and factually. This process can begin with positive body language from when the professional or child, young person or adult first enters the room. For example, Your body should be facing them as you or they enter the room and you should make eye contact comfortably. This is where the professional is not looking around the room, or through their papers but at the child, young person or adult. Arms should be uncrossed to demonstrate that listening is taking place and there are no barriers. Folded arms across the chest can be seen as a barrier to communication and engagement.

ACTIVITY **2.3**

Over a 24-hour period make a list of the different things you have communicated and what methods you used. These could include your communication methods and content at work, college/university and home situations, interactions with friends and people within your community. Examples could be speaking, writing or dressing in a particular way.

How is your chosen method of communication affected by what you wanted to say or what message you wanted to get across and the place/person you are communicating with?

Describe a situation when your communication method brought you success and/or a situation where it prevented you from achieving your aims.

Comment

When we reflect on past interactions, it can be difficult to identify what we did right and wrong and to measure how effective we were but it is important that we do this to develop our communication skills. We should also be aware that some messages sent are not always intentional.

CASE STUDY

At 16.15 hours Sammy knocked on her line manager's open office door and asked for five minutes to discuss something that she is concerned about. He says 'yes, of course' and invites her in.

Sammy started to explain the situation but noticed that Ian kept looking past her towards his open office door. This started to make her feel that Ian did not have the time to listen to her and she cut short her discussion, apologised for taking up his time and said she would think it through herself and maybe catch up with him tomorrow.

Ian may not have consciously realised that he kept looking at his office door while Sammy was talking but he had wanted to catch someone else before they left for the day. But Sammy did notice and it made her feel that Ian had something more important to do than listen to her and therefore she did not finish explaining her concerns.

Developing good listening skills with a child, young person, family, carer or other professional, will support the communication, engagement and information-gathering processes. When the support identified is put in place, having a good relationship with the child, young person, parent and carer can ease the difficulties that can occur, which may affect the success of the interventions. Opportunities to effectively articulate their thoughts, experiences, difficulties and challenges to professionals give children, young people, families and carers a voice in the decision-making process.

Communication within integrated services

Professionals working within integrated services bring with them different practices, terminologies and meanings but they also bring a wide range of skills, knowledge and experience. Difficulties can occur around communication processes; sharing and exchanging information; or when there is a lack of understanding of roles and responsibilities. These are challenges for professionals and agencies required to achieve the aims of *Every Child Matters* (DfES, 2003). Sharing information within integrated services can ensure a child or young person receives the early intervention and services they require (CWDC, 2008).

Children, young people, parents and carers need to have confidence in the professionals they are sharing their story with. The effective implementation and management of the Common Assessment Framework can be the key to provide the evidence that children, young people, parents and carers need to develop confidence in professionals and share information with them. Children, young people, parents and carers are more likely to communicate with professionals who are accessible and approachable and that they trust (Tunstall and Allnock, 2007).

Professionals, working 'effectively and creatively within their own professional areas of expertise, and alongside others from different professions' (Barker, 2009, p. 187) can find the process challenging. Knowledge and understanding of other professional roles and responsibilities within integrated services is essential to overcome some of the barriers.

Integrated services face a wide range of challenges but collaboration around inter-agency communication, where everyone involved is developing a positive attitude to nurturing and sustaining this integration, can overcome the challenge of sharing and exchanging information. This does require ongoing commitment and joined up working by a range of professionals (Tunstall and Allnock, 2007).

Children, young people, parents and carers have a right to be listened to and have their views and opinions taken into account in any decision-making process regarding their lives. Despite this practice being clearly outlined in Every Child Matters and the Children Act 2004, professionals still have a long way to go to ensure everyone is involved in the process.

C H A P T E R   S U M M A R Y

As stated at the beginning of this chapter, communication is a skill and it is not always simple and straightforward to learn and develop. Effective communication requires a professional to practise and continually review their knowledge of and skills in communication and engagement with children, young people, those who care for them and other professionals and be fully aware of the significant change effective communication can bring to these relationships. It is important for a professional to reflect on their skills and then build on them. Issues around miscommunication must be identified and resolved to ensure that every child, young person, parent and carer is given the opportunity to transfer and receive information from professionals.

FURTHER READING

Edwards, A, Daniels, H, Gallagher, T, Leadbetter, J and Warrington, P (2009) *Improving inter-professional collaborations: Multi-agency working for children's wellbeing*. Abingdon: Routledge.

This inter-collaboration text provides the reader with examples from the workplace and provides suggestions of how organisations can work together to support professional practices.

Fitzgerald, D and Kay, J (2008) *Working together in children's services*. Abingdon: Routledge.

Presents a range of theoretical perspectives and contexts of working in a team to support the needs of the child, young person, family and carer.

Chapter 3
Listen to me, please . . .

Kyriaki Messiou

Objectives

By the end of this chapter, you should have an understanding of:

- The importance of listening to the views of children and the links between inclusion and engaging with children's voices.
- The increasing national and international emphasis on engaging with children's voices.
- Various practical ways that can be used to engage with children's voices.
- The challenges associated with listening to children's voices.

Introduction

This chapter aims to explore the concept of listening to children's voices in order to truly make every child matter. First, it will explore how the views of children were absent in the past and how a greater emphasis has been placed on children's voices in recent years in various countries, especially after the UN Convention on the Rights of the Child (UNICEF, 1989). Particular reference will be made to the national context and the emphasis given on children's voices through the *Every Child Matters* (DfES, 2003) agenda. Also, the links between inclusive education, as a concept concerned with any learner that might experience marginalisation within a context, and the idea of listening to children's voices will be explored. Finally, the importance of listening to children will be analysed through the use of particular examples from a research study.

Listening to children's voices

The word 'voices' encompasses the idea of having a say, referring to language and emotional components, as well as non-verbal means that are used to express opinions (Thomson, 2008). Children's voices have traditionally been overlooked, based on the assumption that children were not in a position to provide accurate information, or make judgements, about matters that concern them (Qvortrup, 1994). However, in recent years this view has been changing. This mainly derives from the ways in which childhood is viewed nowadays. For example, many authors (e.g. James et al., 1998; Mills, 2000; Pilcher and Wagg, 1996; Prout and James, 1990) argue that childhood is socially constructed and the child is viewed as a social actor, or in other words the child is viewed as 'being' rather than as 'becoming', where the notion of change and alteration is implied in order for the child to fit into the adults' world. This view of the child is central in the discussion around the notion of listening to children's voices. If children are social actors – as 'being' – with valued views and understandings, then listening to their voices should be an important element of issues that affect them.

In addition to this changing conception of children, the idea of listening to children is now sometimes supported by international documents; for example, it is emphasised in Article 12 of the UN Convention on the Rights of the Child (1989), which reads:

1. States Parties shall assure to the child who is capable of forming his or her own views the right to express those views freely in all matters affecting the child, the view of the child being given due weight in accordance with age and maturity of the child.

2. For this purpose, the child shall in particular be provided with the opportunity to be heard in any judicial and administrative proceedings affecting the child, either directly or through a representative or an appropriate body, in a manner consistent with the procedural rules of natural law.

However, even though Article 12 supports children's right to be heard, the fact that age and maturity of the child are also mentioned leaves a door open for those who had previously rejected this idea precisely for this reason. This is not to deny the role age and maturity play in expressing views, but to emphasise the fact that, regardless of age and maturity, each person's view is equally important.

What is of importance is that the Convention presents a new vision of the child. In this sense, children are neither the property of their parents, nor helpless objects of charity, but are human beings who have their own rights (www.unicef.org/crc/crc.htm).

In England, particular emphasis is given to children's voices through recent policy documents like *Every Child Matters* (DfES, 2003) and *The Children's Plan* (DCFS, 2007). The importance of children's participation in order to achieve the five outcomes of the Every Childs Matters agenda is emphasised in both documents. Through these documents, the government's aim is for every child, regardless of background or circumstances, to have the support they need in order to achieve the following five outcomes:

- Be healthy

- Stay safe

- Enjoy and achieve

- Make a positive contribution

- Achieve economic well-being

In the *Every Child Matters* documentation, it is emphasised that every local authority will be working with its partners, through children's trusts, first, to find out what works best for children and young people in its area and, second, to act on it (www.everychildmatters. gov.uk/aims). In this process children's and young people's involvement is highlighted, with particular reference made to listening to the views of children and young people when inspectors assess the performance of local authorities.

The *Every Child Matters* policy is based on the inquiry into the tragic death of Victoria Climbié, an eight-year-old girl who was abused by her great aunt and her partner, and left to die. Possibly that girl was wishing that someone would listen. Unfortunately, this did not happen. More recently, we have also had other high profile examples of where the system has failed to meet children's needs. Therefore, the argument here is that, in order to truly make every child matter, one way forward is to place greater emphasis on listening to children.

Apart from the general issue of children's right to be heard, what is the value of listening to their views about education? Listening to children's voices is viewed both as an ethical imperative, as well as a matter of practical utility and efficacy (Davie and Galloway, 1996). Charlton (1996) provides a set of reasons why we listen to children in schools. He argues that we listen to children in our effort to know more about them, so as to understand and provide help, or because they need to talk about a concern or fear. He proceeds by saying that we should listen to diagnose problems and therefore help children. Lastly, he points out that we also listen to children because we value their involvement in school affairs and listening to their views is a way to extend our knowledge of their perceptions of those experiences. In doing so, he argues, we might learn more about our successes and failures, and consider possible changes.

Of all the reasons Charlton (ibid.) suggests, I will focus on this last point, about valuing children's perspectives as a way to learn more about our own practices and think about possible changes, as being the most important.

Even though the idea of listening to children's voices is gaining ground, there is a danger that the approach is used in a rather superficial way. Hart (1992) suggests a 'Ladder of Participation', designed to serve as a beginning typology for thinking about the participation of children in projects (see Figure 3.1).

In particular, he identifies eight different levels of young people's participation in projects:

- *Manipulation* – when the adults feel that the end justifies the means. Hart provides an example of preschool children carrying political placards concerning the impact of social policies on children. In this case, children have no understanding of the issues or their actions and therefore this could be described as a way of manipulation.

- *Decoration* – again, when children take part in events organised by adults, and have little understanding about the event or no say in its organisation.

- *Tokenism* – when children are given a voice but have little or no choice about the subject or the style of communicating it. One example is when children are used in conference panels but in a rather superficial way.

- *Assigned but informed* – when children are informed about a situation and then asked to participate in the event.

Figure 3.1 The ladder of participation

Source: Hart, RA (1992) *Children's participation: From tokenism to citizenship*. Innocenti Essays, no. 4. UNICEF International Child Development Centre, Florence (kindly note that the centre is formally known as the International Child Development Centre and the book was published under that imprint).

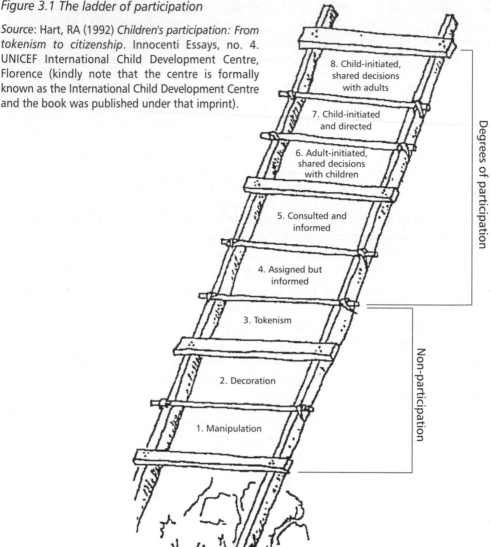

8. Child-initiated, shared decisions with adults

7. Child-initiated and directed

6. Adult-initiated, shared decisions with children

5. Consulted and informed

4. Assigned but informed

3. Tokenism

2. Decoration

1. Manipulation

Degrees of participation

Non-participation

- *Consulted and informed* – where children's views are taken into account in the organising of an event and also informed about the decisions being made.
- *Adult-initiated shared decisions with children* – when a project is started by adults but the decisions are made in collaboration with children.
- *Child-initiated and directed* – when children are the ones to start and direct a project and come up with decisions without involving adults in that process.
- *Child-initiated shared decisions with adults* – when the ideas for a project come from children but they share their decisions with adults in order to organise an event or project.

Hart (ibid.) argues that the main differences between the three lower levels on the ladder, that he labels non-participatory, and the upper five steps, that he labels participatory, is that in all of the upper stages:

- Children understand the intentions of the project.

- Know who made decisions about this involvement and why.

- Volunteer for the project after it is made clear to them what the project is about.

Even though Hart's ladder mainly refers to children's and young people's participation in projects, it can be used as a tool for thinking about the way we engage with children's voices in any context. The idea is to try and include children as much as possible and preferably, where possible, in one of the higher levels of the ladder.

CASE STUDY

Mary is a primary school teacher. She teaches children aged 10–11 years old. As part of her teaching she tries to involve children as much as possible. Recently, she has carried out a project with children where she used visual methods to explore children's views about her teaching practices. In particular, she organised children in groups and gave them digital cameras and asked pupils to take photographs that show what they like doing and what they don't like doing in their class, as well as identify aspects within the class that help or hinder their learning. Eventually, children in their groups had to make posters showing their views and present them to the rest of the class and the teacher. The children came up with very interesting ideas, such as the fact that they like it when they work in groups and the teacher is going around the class helping them; they like it when they are asked to help other children in the class; and they don't like particular lessons and the way they are taught.

- *The children came up with interesting ideas and suggestions, some of which could be described as positive and others as challenging. How should the teacher respond to the most challenging ideas that children came up with in this project? Should the teacher do what the children are suggesting in order to please them?*

- *Think about the children and young people that you know. Do you think that there are any of them, or groups of them, that could not be consulted about matters that affect them? What are the challenges that we might face in trying to gain the voices of some particular groups of children and young people?*

Comment

The idea of listening to children's voices is certainly gaining ground. However, there has been a lot of discussion around particular groups of children and young people, for example very young children and children defined as having special needs. Even though the task of engaging with those particular learners' voices may be more demanding, in finding ways to bring to the surface those learners' voices, nevertheless this should not be used as an excuse for not engaging with those voices. Furthermore, many techniques have been used with children and young people in particular, focusing on enabling them to express their views in the most authentic way. Some of these techniques will be presented and discussed later (for more information, see Further Reading at the end of this chapter).

Also, the issue of responding to what children and young people have said is the most difficult aspect within this process. Certainly, what children and young people express is not necessarily always appropriate. But the idea is that you can use their own voices as a platform for a meaningful discussion through which children and young people, as well as adults, can reflect on their actions and thoughts.

Inclusion and engaging with children's and young people's voices

The term 'inclusion' has various meanings attached to it. Florian (1998) rightly argues that many definitions of inclusion exist and tend to focus on different aspects. Some of the definitions, she argues, focus on human interaction, others on valuing diversity, and others on organisational arrangements. Increasingly, authors view inclusion in much broader terms (e.g. Armstrong et al., 2000; Ballard, 1997; Booth and Ainscow, 1998; Mittler, 2000). In so doing, they explicitly point out that inclusion is concerned with any kind of marginalisation that might be experienced by any child, regardless of whether it is perceived as concerning notions of special needs or not. Ainscow et al. (2006, p. 15) refer to a typology of six ways of thinking about inclusion:

- A concern with disabled students and others categorised as 'having special educational needs'.

- A response to disciplinary exclusion.

- About all groups vulnerable to exclusion.

- The promotion of the school for all.

- 'Education for all.'

- A principled approach to education.

This last formulation, 'a principled approach to education', emphasises the fact that inclusion is a never-ending process concerned with all children and young people, and focuses on their presence, participation and achievement in schools. This approach is also consistent with the broader view of inclusion that was mentioned earlier, one that focuses on all learners.

Similarly, Mittler (2000) defines inclusion as being 'about everyone having opportunities for choice and self-determination. In education, it means listening to and valuing what children have to say, regardless of age or labels' (p. viii). Therefore, it is not just about listening to children's and young people's voices, but going a step further and truly valuing what they have to say. Barton (1997) goes further, defining inclusion as being 'about listening to unfamiliar voices, being open, empowering all members and about celebrating 'difference' in dignified ways. . .. Inclusive experience is about learning to live with one another' (p. 233). Therefore, it could be argued that through this process of listening to children's and young people's voices we are empowering them, as well as recognising that they are valued members of a community. At the same time, though, through this process we are learning to live with one another, which is central to inclusion.

Therefore, taking this broader view of inclusion as being concerned with any learner that might experience marginalisation, the argument here is that in order to truly be inclusive we should take notice of *all* learners' voices. In other words, listening to children's and young people's voices is a manifestation of being inclusive (Messiou, 2006b).

Engaging with children's voices in practice

Engaging with children's voices is a field that has gained lots of attention recently. Various ways to capture children's views in research, as well as in educational settings, are mentioned in the literature (e.g. Ainscow et al., 1999; Allan, 1999; Fielding, 2001; MacBeath et al., 2003; Rudduck and Flutter, 2000). Furthermore, there is a vast number of techniques recommended for use when doing research with children, and especially when interviewing children and young people (e.g. Davis, 2000; Hall and McGregor, 2000; Hazel, 1995; Lewis, 1995, 2002; Mauthner, 1997; O'Kane, 2000; Punch, 2002; Thomas and O'Kane, 1998; Thomson, 2008; Vlachou, 1997). Among those techniques suggested are: using drawings, using images like pictures, photographs, cue cards; using games; and telling stories. The aim of such techniques is to facilitate children's talking, on the one hand, and to make the interview more enjoyable, on the other hand.

Activities 3.1 and 3.2 are based on a study aimed at listening to children's voices in order to understand notions of marginalisation and inclusion. Harden et al. (2000) suggest that research is shaped according to the way in which researchers conceive childhood. This study was developed on the notion that children should be seen as active participants who make sense of their world as they engage with it. Therefore, the approaches used treated children as active participants and not as subjects of the research. (Further details regarding this research and its findings can be found in other publications, e.g. Messiou, 2003, 2006a). Individual interviews were carried out with primary school children and various techniques were used to elicit children's views.

ACTIVITY **3.1**

Message in a bottle is a technique used by Davies (2000) to investigate children's understandings of democratic processes in primary schools. For the purposes of this study (Messiou, 2003, 2006 a/b – see refs), the technique was modified and used as part of the process of individual interviews with primary school children. Children were asked to write or say a message that would be sent to another planet, stating something that they were not happy with at school and would like to change. The aim in the particular research was to bring to the surface possible views of marginalisation.

Some of the messages that emerged were:

I would like others, during playtime, not to beat me or kick me.

I would like the teacher to stop telling me off.

I would like everyone to love me and pay attention to me.

I would like to change school because everyone is making fun of me.

ACTIVITY **3.1** *continued*

I would like other children to play with me.

I would like to be a good pupil.

(Messiou, 2003, 2008)

- *What are the strengths of the above technique?*
- *Can you think of other ways to use this activity?*
- *Do you think that this activity could be used with younger children and/or older children?*
- *What would you do differently for different age ranges?*

Comment

The 'message in a bottle' activity enables children and young people express their views in a way that is not threatening. The technique can be used in a number of different ways. In the above example, the technique has been used as part of interviews where the children were asked at the beginning to say or to write a message that would be sent to another planet what they would like to change in their school if they could change something. The children were given the choice of either say or write down their message, taking into account the differences among children and the fact that some of the children might have difficulties with writing. In the interview process this worked well and many children showed feeling relieved when they were given the option of saying instead of writing the message. However, if you use the message in a bottle idea in a situation where all children are gathered as a group it might be difficult giving them the above option. Therefore, most of the time when the activity is used with a whole group of children they are asked to write down their message. Certainly this might present difficulties for some particular children and young people who might struggle with writing.

In addition to this, if the activity is used with a group of children or young people anonymity is another issue that needs to be considered. The danger is, of course, that if the activity is anonymous then we might not be in a position to identify the concerns of particular children and therefore act on them. On the other hand, if children or young people know that they can be identified, they might not freely express their views. In that case, the issue of confidentiality is what matters and must be clarified to ensure children's understanding of the situation at the beginning of the activity. What is of importance, therefore, is to use the technique in such a way so as to get those children's and young people's views that we might not have been in a position to do in any other way.

Sociograms

Activity 3.2 refers to another technique that was used in the study's individual interviews: the sociogram technique. Sociograms are visual representations of the relationships between all members of a particular group.

ACTIVITY 3.2

As part of individual interviews with a researcher, children were asked to name three classmates they would like to play with and three they would like to work with if they could choose. Children also had to justify their decisions; in other words, give their reasons for choosing the children they chose.

After gathering children's views, their preferences were entered in a table and the relevant sociogram (see Figure 3.2) was developed. Specifically, in a sociogram, individuals are represented as points and the relationships between them as lines with arrows in their end.

- *Moreno (1934) suggests that the sociogram is not just the visual representation of the responses of the participants but, first, is a method for exploration. What is your view? What information can you derive from this sociogram?*

- *How could this be helpful in a given context?*

- *Can you suggest any other ways that the sociogram technique could be used?*

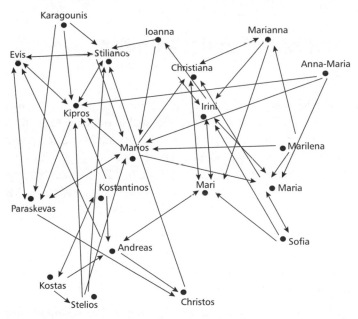

Figure 3.2 A sociogram

Comment

Sociograms are an interesting technique to use with children and young people, and can be used in a number of ways. They can be used with individual children, on a one-to-one basis, as in the above examples. They can also be used with a group of children and young people; here, they are asked to write down their preferences and the adults then tabulate the information and produce a sociogram. If sociograms are going to be used on a one-to-one basis, but when others are present, great care is needed so that the others do not listen to the responses of their friends. This is to avoid the child feeling that somebody has chosen them and therefore they should also choose that person.

It should be noted, however, that even though the sociogram technique can be used to explore social relations among groups of children and young people, it has its drawbacks. In another piece of research that I carried out, using the sociogram technique, one of the children came to see me the next day after her interview to ask me to change her second nomination because she had changed her mind. As I have argued elsewhere, sociograms can provide us only with a rough estimation of children's and young people's preferences, and therefore we should not rely only on them for decisions or judgements that are related to them (Messiou, 2002). Moreno (1934) argues that the sociogram can be used as a method for exploration. In the example that I have used above, children also had to justify their preferences and therefore I could further explore their choices. Furthermore, even without that further justification, the visual representation in itself can provide a useful basis for more in-depth explorations in specific contexts and the social relations among children and young people.

Both the activities – the message in a bottle and the sociogram technique – were used as part of individual interviews with children. However, as mentioned, these techniques, and variations of the techniques, could be used with a whole group of children and young people in a variety of contexts, and not just in schools, in order to listen to children's voices.

Challenges associated with listening to children's voices

Listening to children's voices provides many challenges for those involved. One of the major challenges is for adults to be convinced that there is some potential in listening to children in order to truly engage with their voices in a meaningful way. Unless adults are convinced that they will gain by listening to children, they are not likely to truly engage with their voices other than in tokenistic ways. Morrow and Richards (1996, p. 100) suggest that the biggest ethical challenge for researchers who involve children in their research is the disparities in power and status between adults and children. They argue that:

> *using methods which are non-invasive, non-confrontational and participatory, and which encourage children to interpret their own data, might be one step forward in diminishing the ethical problems of imbalanced relationships between researcher and researched at the point of data collection and interpretation.*

Similarly, engaging with children's and young people's voices in any context entails this difference in terms of power status. The techniques that were described above are seen as simultaneously non-invasive and participatory, breaking this imbalanced relationship between adults and children. But beyond the use of specific techniques, adults should create those conditions that will make children feel confident enough to share their views with them.

In essence, even if there are specific techniques to elicit children's and young people's views, and especially for some children that can be described as more challenging than others, unless they feel that there is an element of trust between them and the adults surrounding them they are not likely to share their views with adults.

Furthermore, if we are talking about research, the issue of gaining consent is another challenge. As Thomas and O' Kane (1998) argue, this is complicated by the fact that both adults' and children's consent is required. In reality, unless you have the adults' consent, not least that of the parents, you cannot move on to request children's consent. In this sense, children's choice of whether or not to participate in research is limited. Thomas and O'Kane (ibid.) go on to argue that another ethical issue, which is more problematic in research with children, is that of confidentiality, since there might be adults who expect to be told about the thoughts of children for whom they are responsible.

Another challenge is that the process is not necessarily straightforward. So, for example, Ainscow and Kaplan (2005) refer to a school where adults denied that what their children were expressing about their school was the truth. They provide an account of where the comments from students suggested that their involvement in decisions about a new uniform was rather tokenistic, something that the teachers described as untrue. On the contrary, the senior team saw student involvement in decision making as one of the strengths of the school and how they were running it.

Therefore, this process of listening to students' voices might evoke tensions and feelings of uncertainty among adults in relation to their own actions. However, this should not be viewed as a reason for not engaging with students' voices. On the contrary, it should be viewed as a challenge and a risk in itself. The important point of this example is not whether the students were lying or being truthful, but that they were expressing how they felt. In that context, therefore, members of staff who felt that what the students said was untrue should take it as an opportunity to explore why those students felt the way they felt and investigate ways to engage in dialogues with the students about what is happening in school.

Lastly, and most importantly, is the issue of dealing with the issues that might emerge through listening to children's voices. As I have argued elsewhere (Messiou, 2006b), listening to children's voices should go beyond simply listening and move on to taking action. Roberts (2000) argues that listening to children, hearing children and acting on what they say are three very different activities. I would say that the most challenging activity is acting on what children have expressed.

C H A P T E R   S U M M A R Y

The title of this chapter is 'Listen to me, please . . .'. Possibly Victoria Climbié was making this wish in her prayers. We will never know. What we do know is that there are possibly other children out there who have that wish, not necessarily because they are abused but because they feel a desire to express their points of view. Therefore, we should aim to move away from children having to ask for this right to a situation where listening to their voices becomes a necessary process in any context that seeks to involve children and young people.

Thomson, P (2008) *Doing visual research with children and young people*. London: Routledge.

Visual methods are a potentially powerful and, recently very popular, way of engaging with children's and young people's voices. This book explores methodological, ethical as well as theoretical issues that relate to image-based research with children and young people. It also provides useful ideas from various research projects about how to use visual images with children and young people in order to listen to their voices.

Christensen, P and James, A (2001) *Research with children: Perspectives and practices*. London: RoutledgeFalmer.

This book provides useful examples from research with children and addresses important methodological issues. The examples come from a range of disciplines including sociology, anthropology, psychology, history, education and social policy and practice.

DCSF (2008) *Working together: Listening to the voices of children and young people*. London: DCSF.

This Government document provides guidance about how to encourage participation of children and young people in decision-making in schools, local authorities and other settings. It explores the definition of participation, and the benefits of children's and young people's participation for further improvement. It also provides interesting examples of putting the principle of participation into practice.

www.consultingpupils.co.uk

www.unicef.org.uk

Chapter 4

Children's voices: Working with children and young people with additional needs

Eileen Wake

Objectives

By the end of this chapter, you should have an understanding of:

- Communication when working with children and young people with a wide range of additional needs.

- The importance of emotional well-being and the development of emotional intelligence and resilience.

- Communication issues and problems that children with disabilities may encounter in making their needs, choices and feelings known.

Introduction

This chapter has sought to explore the importance of communication when working with children and young people with a wide range of additional needs. Every child is unique and this chapter offers a snapshot into some of the many complex issues that need to be considered when working with children and young people. The first section of the chapter explores the importance of emotional well-being and the development of emotional intelligence and resilience. The potential reasons why a child/young person may be more vulnerable to developing mental health problems are considered and two specific mental health problems that a child/young person may experience: eating disorders and self-harm. Listening for as well as to children and young people is also discussed. Resources to help the reader understand how they can help vulnerable children and young people are identified.

The second half of the chapter, in contrast, specifically explores some of the communication issues and problems that children with disabilities may encounter in making their needs, choices and feelings known. Specific issues for children and young people with sensory impairments and also autistic spectrum disorders have been explored. The value of augmentative and alternative communication is considered and the reader offered practical advice regarding how to develop their communication skills further.

The mental health needs of children and young people

The emotional well-being of children and young people is often overlooked or explained in behavioural terms according to their development or an adult perspective of their responses in given situations, such as within school. As adults, however, we expect others to listen to us and take on board our feelings and concerns; why, then, do we not do this for children and young people? The Office for National Statistics (2005) identified that one in ten children and young people have clinically identified mental health problems. Indeed BEAT, the national charity supporting people with eating disorders, recently highlighted that the incidence of eating disorders in young people is increasing (2009a, 2009b), as is the incidence of self-harm amongst young people, as highlighted by Hawton et al. (2006). Worryingly, a review of ChildLine by Brookes (2009) for the NSPCC identified that the number of children and young people accessing it for support has tripled in the past five years, with at least one in 16 of the children and young people expressing suicidal intentions being under the age of 11. For the purpose of this chapter only, the term self-harm is used to define those children and young people who intentionally self-harm but are 'reasonably secure . . . that death will not result from their action' (Kerfoot, 2001, p. 112) – often more commonly termed as deliberate self-harm.

Both are conditions that are based upon feelings, emotions and a need to feel in control of their lives (Royal College of Psychiatrists, 2004). The reasons why children and young people may, for example, self-harm or develop an eating disorder are complex and multi-factorial, including individual (personality, coping mechanisms, cognitive skills), family systems (stressful family relationships), life events (bereavement or severe illness), life choices and expectations, as well as social factors. There is a consistent message in relation to all aspects of mental health, including the two conditions explored in this chapter – that of emotional well-being, emotional literacy, emotional resilience and the development of cognitive and age-appropriate coping mechanisms.

Therefore it is important that we develop a sound working understanding of emotional intelligence – that of children and young people, and of our own, as at times professionals may perpetuate a problem inadvertently due to their own limited communication and emotional intelligence skills, as highlighted by Carr (2000, 2006).

Goleman (1995, 2005) proposed that our emotions serve many purposes in our everyday lives and help us to identify and communicate when our basic human needs (within Maslow's (1998) hierarchy of needs) are or are not being met. Indeed, Hein (2007) highlighted the importance of the development of 'healthy feelings', focusing upon the emotions that we want to feel and how one reaches them. Emotions such as anger are what Goleman (1995, 2005), Zelman et al. (2006) and Hein (2007) cite as being secondary and thus more intense emotions, which arise in relation to primary emotions such as feeling overwhelmed, isolated or scared by an event/experience. Therefore practitioners working with children and young people need to be able to work therapeutically in partnership with a child/young person to explore why and where these feelings arise. They need to be able to work with them and provide practical support such as sources of help when they feel distressed or worried, as well as aid in the development of positive coping mechanisms when they are exposed to difficult situations in the future.

Recognition of the significance of this is important in order to understand children and young people and, indeed, our own responses to situations/events or people; it is when emotional needs are not being met, for example the need to feel safe, loved and cared for (Barlow and Underdown, 2005), that difficulties can arise. These difficulties can present in a child/young person using inappropriate and/or immature coping mechanisms, which may be misinterpreted as difficult or risk-taking behaviours by others. This does not necessary result in the use of more problematic coping strategies, however; this may manifest itself for some particularly vulnerable children and young people in them cutting themself to channel feelings such as frustration and isolation. Unfortunately, then, cutting or other forms of self-harm may become a learnt coping mechanism and one that the young person may use more and more in order to feel in control of the situation or unwanted feelings.

CASE STUDY

Darren is 15. To everyone who meets him, he appears outgoing, happy and a great help to his family. Darren's younger sister Marie (aged 13) has a life-limiting condition. However, at school Darren has been not attending and not handing in his homework on time; his marks for his work have deteriorated. Darren has been taking prescribed painkillers for persistent headaches every day for the last year.

* *Why do you think Darren's school attendance and work are a problem?*

* *Why do you think Darren has been having problems with headaches for this length of time?*

Comment

The scenario above is designed for the reader to consider the wide range of potential issues that affect our everyday behaviours and to reflect upon the notion of roles we are expected to play in families and the potential problems this can have for young people. In order to understand Darren's behaviour, the reader needs to reflect upon the whole situation from his developmental perspective, that of a 15 year old, and try to avoid assumptions based on observable behaviour.

Wanting to feel loved, cared for, part of a group yet valued as an individual, are all important and powerful emotions. Goleman (1995, 2005) described these in terms of survival emotions, in that those feelings of loneliness and being ignored stem from a need to feel part of a group, to feel connected with others. This is an important developmental step for children and young people– wanting to be part of the group, wanted and accepted; this is highlighted in Erickson's (1965) seminal work and supported by, for example, Dowling

(2005), O'Hagan (2006), Santrock (2007) and Hantler (2008) and explored recently in the work by Stevens (2008). This stems from attachment behaviour of infants with their primary carer(s) and the resultant bonding, identified in seminal research by Bowlby (1965, 1969, 1979, 1988), and further by Ainsworth et al. (1978) in relation to how infants respond in new situations. However, there is much discussion regarding what can and cannot be inferred from the behaviour of infants and children as attachment behaviours, as attachment happens over a period of time and does not mean that the child has to show the behaviours associated with attachment all the time (Cassidy and Shaver, 2008). Indeed, there has been much debate regarding attachment theory and an ongoing discourse in relation to the original studies, as well as later studies, and their application in a wider variety of settings. Importantly, the role of fathers and attachment, as well as the impact of differing parenting styles and stressful situations (e.g. Cassidy and Shaver, 2008; Marvin and Brittner, 1995; Prior, 2006; Stevenson-Hinde and Versheuren, 2002), has been explored in a number of studies (see Further Reading at the end of this chapter).

On reviewing the literature to date in relation to communication, it is sufficient to say that readers need to develop a greater understanding of initial attachments and the resultant significance of the quality of attachment experienced by children that they are working with. Thus it is important for practitioners working with children who have potential problems related to attachment, to reflect upon the child's life story even if they are now an adolescent, as attachment issues from early childhood can continue to have an impact, as noted by Prior (2006). This should also include exploring parenting style and abilities and the way in which the primary carer(s) has responded to the infant/young child in relation to daily routines. Potential areas where primary carer(s) may have difficulties, for example in managing mealtimes with toddlers, toilet training, night waking and night terrors, also need examining. This is particularly important as practitioners need to be able to utilise therapeutic communication skills when working with parents and be able to explore and identify when behaviours in the child may be reflecting problems in the parent–child relationship, rather than assuming that the issues belong to the child (Keren et al., 2001; Robinson, 2002).

The way in which significant adults interact with children and young people has a profound impact on the development of their self-worth and self-esteem. This is demonstrated, for example, in the way children and young people feel about making decisions and choices in everyday life. A sense of success and pleasure when making the right choices reinforces self-worth and self-esteem and that in turn builds upon the child/young person's confidence to make decisions and to trust their own actions. Coupled with positive adult responses to their decisions, this helps them feel confident in future choices and helps them to develop positive developmentally appropriate coping mechanisms. These are essential to help them when the decision they have made doesn't work out and to feel their opinions matter, to feel valued and not ridiculed for the choices they have tried to make. This is an important element of the development of emotional resilience in the child/young person.

However, some children and young people may experience constant exaggerated criticism or be belittled for the decisions they make; they may be made to feel a failure and their decisions judged on adult behaviours and knowledge rather than what is developmentally appropriate. In addition where poor/inappropriate/immature coping mechanisms as highlighted by Carr (2006) are used by parents/carers/significant others, this can create difficulties in terms of emotional development from these learnt behaviours (Bandura, 1977;

Kumpulainen and Wray, 2001). Thus, when working with children and young people in relation to their emotional development and mental health needs, it is important to look at the family as a whole in terms of family functioning, decision making and coping mechanisms used, as advocated by Spender et al. (2001).

However, it is important not to just focus upon family functioning. For the school-aged child the significant others, as Ding (2005) identified, are often the child's teachers and staff in the school setting. If the child feels that their work or behaviour is constantly being criticised in this environment, they do not feel valued; this can also impact upon their self-esteem and self-worth. Thus the child who is exhibiting such problems has a number of unmet emotional needs, which results in the child expressing themselves using learnt coping mechanisms that may not be appropriate – such as behavioural difficulties, bullying or school refusal. Unfortunately the child may then be inadvertently labelled as being difficult and behaviours become assessed from this perspective rather than looking holistically at the child, family and the school environment, as Bronfenbrenner's (2005) ecological model of child development highlights. Therefore when working with children/young people it is important to consider the whole situation from a bio-psychosocial perspective, which can be aided by the use of the Common Assessment Framework (DCSF, 2007b). However, it is important to highlight that, when assessing a child's emotional well-being and resilience, the practitioner remains open to all potential dimensions and not to infer a level of resilience just because that is what they assume the child has. This is supported in a recent study of social workers by McMurray et al. (2008), which identified the importance of in-depth objective assessment and being aware of judgement bias and the potential influence this has on the level of support put in place for children and young people.

CASE STUDY

Paula, aged ten, is considered to be disruptive at school; she struggles to concentrate on her work for any length of time and is inattentive during lessons. This is supported by her parents. The educational team thus feel that Paula perhaps has an attention deficit disorder and arrangements are made for a range of assessments.

However, during one of the assessments Paula discloses that she is worried about her mum as her dad has been hitting her a lot. Paula said she didn't tell her teacher as her mum told her not to.

Comment

This scenario demonstrates the importance of looking beyond the behaviours of the child/young person, to reflect upon the impact of life events from their perspective, acknowledge that they do experience stress, and reflect upon the importance of emotional literacy and resilience in relation to the stress experienced. The stress a child experiences will depend on the way in which they perceive the event/experience, which is affected by their developmental understanding of what has happened or is happening. It is affected by how the child views the situation, for example as harmful or not, and this is influenced by their past experiences, the circumstances prior, during and after the experience and the way in which significant others such as parents/carers/teachers respond to the child and the situation (Brom et al., 2008; Carr, 2000; Maud, 2002; Rutter and Taylor, 2002; Scott et al., 2001).

Practitioners need to be mindful of the potential problem of sensory overload from the experience and the resultant potential flashbacks to events that the child may experience; these affect their ability to cope with situations and/or experiences later in their childhood and indeed into adulthood (Brom et al., 2008). This is a particular issue for younger children who may not have the cognitive skills to be able to comprehend what has happened. They may experience more frequent and distressing flashbacks to events, yet not be able to verbally communicate these with parents/carers. They may demonstrate their distress in physical behaviours, such as regression in self-help skills, and also through play (Spender et al., 2001; Talge et al., 2008; Trapolini et al., 2007).

Why are some children more vulnerable to mental health problems?

The reasons why some children and young people do not develop protective mental health factors – such as positive developmentally mature coping mechanisms and strategies, positive self-esteem and self-worth are – are complex and multi-factorial. The reader is advised to review more specialist sources in order to develop their understanding further (see Further Reading). However, given the increasing numbers of children and young people who are experiencing mental health problems (Department of Health (DoH), 2004b), an overview of some of the problems that practitioners working with children and young people may encounter is relevant. It can be difficult to identify when a particular mental health issue has arisen for a child/young person due to the cognitive, biological and emotional changes as a child develops. Thus it is important that practitioners have a sound understanding of 'normal' developmental processes and milestones before seeking to understand mental health needs. It is also important, however, that practitioners do not make assumptions in relation to a child/young person's behaviour and generalise that it is 'just part of growing up'. There is a significant difference between feeling down and struggling with a particular element of one's life; for example, a relationship problem in adolescence and that of depression. Indeed, Herbert and Harper Dorton (2001) highlighted that problems with loneliness, low self-esteem and peers are unfortunately relatively common (although this does not make them any less important or upsetting for the young person).

However, consistently low self-worth, insomnia, irritability, dysphoria (feeling unhappy), loss of appetite and weight loss are more serious symptoms that can indicate depression in the child or young person. This may manifest itself also in behaviours such as school refusal, being uncharacteristically aggressive (Carr, 2006; Herbert and Harper Dorton, 2001) or risk taking, and it is important that practitioners recognise that depression is not exclusively a problem for young people and adults but can occur in children too, although much less commonly (Rethink, 2009). However, practitioners also need to be aware that undiagnosed underlying chronic health problems can also result in some of the symptoms cited above and thus it is important that a child/young person is reviewed by a paediatrician to identify or rule out any underlying health problem rather than assume that mental health problems are evident.

Eating disorders: all about feelings

The importance of ensuring that any underlying physical health problem is excluded is essential for conditions such as eating disorders. A common misperception about eating disorders is that they are all about food and a preoccupation with being excessively slim; however, these are just the symptoms of eating disorders such as anorexia nervosa and bulimia – the real focus of the problem is feelings and the child/young person may judge their worth and success in terms of how they are able to control their weight and therefore their feelings (BEAT, 2009a, 2009b; McNamara et al., 2008). Feelings of low self-esteem, unworthiness, being unable to control one's daily life and failure are all examples of unmet emotional needs, which are part of the complex nature of eating disorders for children and young people. There are many triggers that may result in a child/young person developing an eating disorder, including significant life events/pressures such as bereavement, family break-up and being bullied. For some vulnerable children/young people whose self-esteem and self-worth are low and who have struggled with developing positive coping mechanisms, difficulties with friendships and peer pressure can all exacerbate feelings of unworthiness and exacerbate their perception of their body image and of being not in control of their daily life. Restricting calorific intake and restricting where, who with and when you eat is an attempt to regain this control. Practitioners must be aware of the need for sensitivity and support for children when undertaking any child health surveillance, such as weight and height (National Institute for Health and Clinical Excellence (NICE), 2006), given the likelihood of low self-esteem/self-worth in children experiencing body image issues. Practitioners again need to have a sound understanding of bio-psychosocial development for the age group and to be aware of the signs and symptoms that may give concern when working with children and young people, some of which may be similar to depression (indeed a child/young person with an eating disorder may also be depressed).

If concerned, the practitioner needs to work in partnership with the child/young person and their family and refer to health care practitioners for further advice and follow up; the usual first contact is the school nurse for the school and the general practitioner. Clear, consistent communication (including written elements) between everyone involved with and for the child/young person is essential to ensure that they have access to the help they need at the right time. Indeed NICE (2004a) stressed that it is essential that referral for such support is made as early as possible, as this will increase the likelihood of successful outcomes of the therapeutic strategies needed It is important that all practitioners supporting the child/young person with an eating disorder work with the family as a whole, including siblings where appropriate (ibid.), to ensure support is in place in relation to parenting issues such as meal times, which can and do have an impact on family functioning on a day-to-day basis. Involvement of an appropriate support group such as Beat can be an excellent source of additional help for the family during this difficult time.

Deliberate self-harm

Self-harm is defined by NICE (2004b, p. 5) as: 'self poisoning or injury, irrespective of the apparent purpose of the act. It is an expression of personal distress, not an illness, and there are many varied reasons for a person to harm him or herself.' It is important that practitioners work with this definition, as it also includes alcohol ingestion, which is significant in terms of the binge drinking culture that is prevalent in the UK (Parliamentary Office of Science and Technology, 2005), and its impact on the increasing number of young people who have difficulties in their lives due to their alcohol consumption (Martinic and Measham, 2008). Deliberate self-harm has developmental, gender and situational influences regarding what particular form of deliberate self-harm is used. This includes a wide variation of acts, for example: cutting, pulling out hair, biting, burning, self-strangulation, self-poisoning and substance misuse.

The complexity of this area concerns all practitioners working with children. Knowing how to support the child/young person appropriately can be daunting: if the seriousness of the intention to self-harm is not fully understood or acted upon the results can be catastrophic. Ongoing open communication and sharing of concerns regarding the welfare of a child/young person appropriately is thus essential. It is estimated that one in 15 young people self-harm (Clements et al., 2008; NSPCC, 2009) and this number is increasing. The average age is considered to be 12 years, but primary school-age children also feature (Clements et al., 2007; Mental Health Foundation, 2006).

Self-harm is often misunderstood by the public, and indeed professionals. Practitioners must access support and guidance from specialist workers within child and adolescent mental health (CAMH) self-harm teams; they can provide advice regarding prevention, early identification and referral to appropriate services. A child or young person who is self-harming must be reviewed by a paediatrician and specialist CAMH workers to ensure their well-being and safety needs are met; this is especially so when concern exists that the self-harm is in response to emotional, physical and/or sexual harm experienced by the child/young person.

When a child/young person repeatedly deliberately self-harms, harm minimisation strategies may be explored by specialist practitioners, alongside other therapeutic interventions. These could include the development of alternative appropriate coping strategies when the young person has harmed by cutting, for example. However, this is not appropriate when the young person has deliberately self-harmed through poisoning, such as an overdose of medication, as no safe limit exists for such a behaviour (NICE, 2004b).

So why do children/young people deliberately self-harm? As with eating disorders, the reasons why they do so are complex and linked to feelings of self-worth and self-esteem, pressure to do well educationally, being bullied, and physical, emotional and sexual harm (NSPCC, 2008). Self-harm is 'always a sign of something being seriously wrong' (Royal College of Psychiatrists, 2004, p. 1). It should always be taken seriously; even if cuts are small or trivial, the fact that they have been inflicted is what matters. They are expressions of feelings of isolation, helplessness or inner unbearable tension; of being out of control and a desire to feel more in control of their lives. However, deliberate self-harm can also be undertaken by the child/young person to punish themselves for an actual or perceived situation/experience that they feel ashamed about or, sadly, as a way of repressing feelings linked to events they have experienced, such as sexual harm (NSPCC, 2007, 2008). Thus, once again, it is about feelings; practitioners need to ensure that they focus on this aspect more when working with children/young people who may have self-harmed and do not communicate negative feelings to them regarding how they themselves view the situation or dismiss the situation by seeing the cut rather than the feelings.

How can you help?

As stated above, working with a child/young person who has deliberately self-harmed can be rather daunting. It is important that medical help is sought to address the manifestation of the deliberate self-harm, e.g. self-poisoning or cutting. It is especially important that immediate help is sought when self-poisoning is suspected as some treatment options involve time limits; the long-term effects on the body of paracetamol overdose cannot be underestimated, for example (Medicines and Healthcare Products Regulatory Body (MHRA), 2009).

In terms of general help, aside from immediate medical aid, it is important that you stay calm and try to avoid focusing on your own feelings about the situation and concentrate on those of the child/young person instead. It is essential that you actively listen to them. You need to take the child/young person's worries/concerns seriously and listen to them in a non-judgemental and empathic way. It will require you to think about your own communication skills and how you can recognise a child/young person's emotional distress and seek to reassure them that their feelings matter and that you are there to help them. You will always need to refer to appropriate health professionals, as cited above; however, you can help and comfort the child/young person, including providing practical advice and support regarding problem solving. In some instances, you may need to enact appropriate procedures for safeguarding children immediately (Laming, 2009; NSPCC, 2008).

All practitioners need to have excellent communication skills to ensure that children/young people who are vulnerable are identified and receive the support that they need. Their parents and siblings must also be supported and communicated with to ensure family functioning. Poor communication by practitioners can mean that children and young people with mental health needs may not be identified or receive the help that they need; they may even deteriorate if a long time elapses before help is received. Always be objective and do not assume that a child/young person is resilient and coping with the situation or their feelings.

It is also important that practitioners address their own mental health needs and communicate their own stress and difficulties with colleagues and their manager/placement mentor/supervisor. A practitioner who is exhausted and stressed may struggle to communicate their workload difficulties, which may mean their clients are not receiving the level of support that they need (Hughes, 2009).

Augmentative and alternative communication – what it is and why it matters

This section considers the communication needs and resultant issues for children/young people with a range of additional needs. Children are children first and foremost, and one could argue that communication issues lie more with practitioners' ability to effectively communicate than with the children. However, poor communication can have a profound impact on a child's ability to make their needs and feelings known and for their wishes to be understood and respected. The resultant frustration that a child/young person may experience can create significant problems, for example regarding choices regarding everyday living, health, education and social issues, self-esteem and self-worth.

Incidence of children with sensory impairment

A Royal National Institute for the Deaf (RNID, 2005) survey identified that approximately 840 infants are born annually with significant hearing impairment in the UK; with one in 1,000 children having a hearing impairment by the age of three years and approximately 20,000 children under 15 years having a moderate to severe hearing impairment. In addition, the RNID survey highlighted that there are approximately 23,000 people in the UK who have hearing and visual impairment; it does not, however, specify the numbers of children and young people within this total.

In relation to visual impairment, the statistics are also hard to identify in terms of a true representation of incidence. The most recent national surveys (by Rahi and Cable, 2003) and the RNIB (2008) only include those children and young people with the most severe form of visual impairment; estimates thus vary from 7,000 to 25,000 in the UK (Bone and Meltzer, 1989; Clunies-Ross, 1997; Keil, 2003).

Augmentative and alternative communication

Communication in the form of talking is more than just speech itself. It involves non-verbal elements such as gesture, facial expression and body posture, as well as acknowledgement of the social context in which the communication is taking place. For a number of children who have sensory impairment and/or learning disabilities, the expression of their wishes using the spoken word may be problematic. It may also include difficulties with understanding; for example, a child with a severe autistic spectrum disorder may have difficulties comprehending words alone (hyperlexia) in written text but may be helped greatly by the introduction of pictures with the words to enhance understanding. Thus, for these children, the use of augmentative and alternative communication systems (alternative only in the sense that each child/young person may need specific communication aids/support to meet their individual needs) may be necessary. Augmentative communication, as highlighted by Millar and Scott (2003), is a term representing a range of strategies, including Touch talkers and picture boards, and electronic tools which can respond to facial movement. These tools are used to enhance communication when a child has difficulty expressing their needs even with gestures and symbols.

Children with sensory impairments such as significant hearing or speech problems may utilise signing as part of their communication alongside or instead of lip reading. Signing should always be accompanied with the spoken word to enhance understanding. Concern has been voiced that the use of signing impacts on a hearing impaired child's ability to develop the spoken word; however, it has actually been found to enhance speech (Robbins, 2002; Swanwick and Tsverik, 2007) if used alongside it. Use of both signing and speech helps the child make their feelings/needs/choices known so that decisions are not made without consulting them. In addition, lip reading is difficult to learn and relies on extra cues such as gestures and facial expressions. Additional problems such as background noise may also have a negative impact on a child/young person's ability to make use of any residual hearing or to maximise the effect of a hearing aid.

For people with hearing impairments who need to utilise additional communication strategies, the most well-known signing system used in the UK is British Sign Language (BSL). According to the RNID (2005), it is used accompanying speech by approximately 50,000 people in the UK as their primary means of communication (although the actual number of children and young people using BSL is not stated). Given these statistics, it is concerning that there are limited numbers of people who are able to translate BSL for people with hearing impairment as highlighted by the RNID (2005). It is important that practitioners gain a good basic understanding of the key elements of BSL and know how to access such support for children and young people in their care. However, practitioners need to be aware that BSL is not internationally used and there are many variations used across the world and indeed also regional variations in the UK just as there are with speech and dialect. BSL is complex and sometimes signs/gestures are similar but are accompanied by different lip patterns (RNID, 2007, 2009). Finger spelling is often used but is only a small part of BSL. Learning BSL is best achieved by attending a course. The RNID website provides lots of information on BSL and the rudiments of finger spelling.

For children with significant hearing and/or speech problems who also have a learning disability, the BSL may be too complex. Here, a simplified method of signing using speech and facial expressions would be more effective. The most well known of these approaches is Makaton™ which uses signs, symbols and speech together, in a highly visual manner. The system is very flexible and includes a wide range of every day vocabulary to develop and enhance communication for all children as part of their development of verbal communication. It is also suitable for children and young people, including those with specific language difficulties and children/young people with autistic spectrum disorder.

Makaton™ focuses on language used in everyday life and utilises signs (gestures) and/or symbols (pictures) dependent on the needs of the child/young person; gestures are often much easier to use and express for a child/young person with a learning disability. The use of pictures symbolising a spoken word, e.g. mum, cup, drink, hungry, is particularly useful for the child/young person who has limited physical movement and would find gesturing difficult; parents/carers/significant others may also potentially misinterpret such gestures. See Figure 4.1.

Scope (2009) provides an invaluable tool for helping understand the communication needs of particular children and young people with profound and multiple disabilities. It enables the practitioner to assess the child/young person's strengths and abilities relating to a wide range of everyday activities and then to adapt strategies accordingly. See the SCOPE website for details.

53

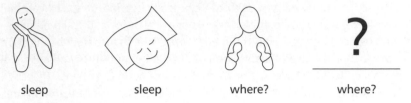

| sleep | sleep | where? | where? |

Figure 4.1 Examples of signs and symbols used by Makaton™

Makaton™ symbol and sign graphics © The Makaton™ Charity (www.makaton.org). Used with permission of the The Makaton™ Charity.

However, there are some problems with the use of gestures and symbols in that they often focus more on the practicalities of every day living, which is understandable. However, there is a need for children/young people to be able to express their feelings and communication toolkits often do not address this effectively and there have also been concerns as highlighted by Marchant and Cross (2002) that the lack of diversity in the symbols and/or gestures makes it more difficult for the child/young person to express their distress in terms of physical, emotional and/or sexual harm. Yet it is recognised that children and young people with disabilities are more vulnerable to harm and/or neglect (National Working Group on child protection and disability (2003); Morris 2006). 'How it is' was launched by Marchant and Cross (2002) on behalf of the NSPCC and Triangle which includes a range of symbols and gestures alongside words in 5 key categories that include:

- Feelings
- Rights and safety
- General vocabulary
- Personal care
- Sexuality

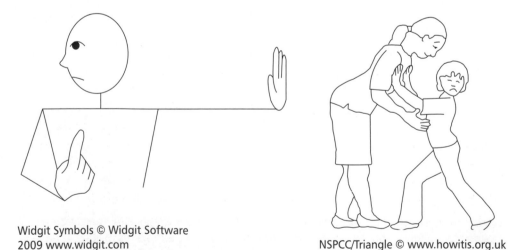

Widgit Symbols © Widgit Software
2009 www.widgit.com

NSPCC/Triangle © www.howitis.org.uk

Figure 4.2 Two versions of picture signs used in Howitis™ that can be used by the child to say: 'Leave me alone, go away, get lost, get off.'

The Makaton charity has now also developed 150 gestures/symbols to use with Makaton™ in relation to sexual health and body parts. This need for the development of a more extensive range of symbols and gestures has been highlighted in a recent survey by Mencap (2007): 93 per cent of all children with learning disabilities are bullied and are twice more likely to be bullied at school than other children. Mencap has since developed a high profile campaign entitled: 'Don't Stick It' to raise awareness of the problem. It uses animation together with gestures and symbols to help children/young people with learning disabilities to express their feelings and experiences of bullying.

Gestures and symbols are obviously ineffective for sight impaired children. Communication with children with severe visual impairment emphasises use of any residual vision as well as maximised use of the other senses, such as touch and hearing. Hence, for children with visual impairment, a number of communication strategies are used, including Braille. The actual numbers of children with visual impairment are difficult to quantify in the UK. This is exacerbated by the limited and patchy availability of vision screening for children, as highlighted by Guggenheim and Fairbrother (2005) and a recent review of provision via primary health care trusts by McLaughlan (2009) for the RNIB. There is an over-reliance on parents/carers, having identified problems affecting the child's behaviour, taking their child to the health visitor, GP or optician for vision testing. This is despite an acknowledgement that untreated refractive errors (vision problems such as short and long sightedness) can cause significant visual impairment that could perhaps be avoided if identified earlier (World Health Organisation, 2000). The RNIB (2008) estimates that approximately 25,000 children have severe visual impairments in the UK; of this number, 12,000 children have additional disabilities (DfES, 2004; Rahi and Cable, 2003).

It is thus vital to maintain, where possible, the child/young person's residual vision and practitioners need to ensure that visual spatial elements are considered; for example, making distinctive contrasts between objects to enable the child to select what they want unaided. It is also important that practitioners do not, as with children with hearing impairment, equate visual or other sensory impairments with learning disabilities. They should communicate with the child/young person in a developmentally appropriate manner, and make contact with them first rather than automatically communicating with the parent/carer. Speech is essential to communication and practitioners need to be mindful of their tone of voice and clarity of speech, and aware that the child/young person will not be able to identify the subtle cues in communication offered by non-verbal elements such as facial expression.

For the child/young person with hearing and visual impairment (dual sensory impairment) for whom Braille is not appropriate, the Moon system may be used (SenseScotland, 2008). This is a communication method similar to Braille but is much easier to grasp and use. The reader is advised to explore the SENSE website for additional information on communication strategies and working with children/young people with dual sensory impairment.

Children with multiple sensory impairment

An additional element to consider in reflecting upon communication strategies is the needs of children with profound and multiple sensory impairment. When a child has a severe visual and hearing impairment alongside other disabilities, it is important to utilise the senses of touch and smell to the full. Communication with children with multiple sensory impairments can be enhanced by the use of non-verbal strategies, for example body signs and objects of reference; these use actual objects as terms of reference to enhance communication – a low technology solution. For the child who has a severe visual impairment in addition to other impairments, such as severe hearing loss, actual objects or miniature versions could be used as cues for the activity that the practitioner wishes to engage in with the child/young person. An example would be tooth brushing. Rather than just undertaking this task with the child/young person, the practitioner could use a toothbrush and toothpaste (the child's favourite or one that has a distinctive smell) and a cup and let the child/young person touch, feel and smell the objects. The involvement of the child/young person in all aspects of the activity in accordance with their developmental skills is crucial. Breaking the activity down into small stages will also help, as the child/young person may have particular worries about, for example, having the brush put in their mouth and assumptions may be made that the child doesn't like having their teeth brushed rather than just that one aspect of the process. If the child as an infant experienced intensive medical interventions, for example oral suction, due to health problems, this can mean that they now associates objects in their mouth with distress; practitioners thus need to be receptive and responsive to the child's communication and use strategies such as desensitisation through play to overcome this particular problem.

For the child who has no additional or limited visual problems but has a significant hearing impairment and a learning disability, using speech, gesture and/or a symbol can act as a strong visual cue as to what you would like to do. Photographs of the objects with the word underneath can also be very useful, especially where the practitioner wants to encourage the child to choose what activity to do next. They can also be used for smaller but no less important choices such as requesting a drink and choosing their favourite cup, which people take for granted but rather like to do.

It is important to stress, as reinforced by Millar and Scott (2003), that there are always ways and means of enabling communication for a child, no matter how complex and profound their disability. If a child has significant issues with visual spatial awareness alongside severe physical and learning disabilities, it is still possible to adapt the communication aids accordingly. The only limits are the communication skills of parents/carers/professionals not the child/young person! Therefore a child may need to utilise different communication strategies which are personalised to meet their own needs. This approach is more commonly known as a total communication system, or total augmentative communication, and needs to be understood and shared with the family and all carers/significant adults who work with the child/young person.

Communicating with children and young people with autistic spectrum disorder

It is difficult to quantify the actual numbers of children and young people with autistic spectrum disorder (ASD), however it is estimated that there are approximately 110,000 children and young people in the UK with conditions such as Asperger's syndrome and 26,000 children and young people in the UK with ASD and a learning disability (Williams et al., 2006). There are some rare conditions which can result in misdiagnosis of ASD however, for example Retts Syndrome, in which the child progressively loses the functional abilities of their hands and develops a number of stereotypical hand movements (Weaving et al., 2005). Obtaining a clear diagnosis, especially in early childhood, can therefore be difficult.

The range and complexities in the form of ASD a child/young person may have are immense and vary from individual to individual. It is important to acknowledge that a diagnosis of ASD does not necessarily mean that the child/young person has a learning disability as well, for example children and young people with Asperger's syndrome. However, what children/young people with ASD do have in common with each other are communication problems and difficulties in relating to others; however, this too varies greatly from child to child. This affects the child's ability to make and sustain friendships, to understand situations from another person's perspective (empathy) and to interpret the subtle nature of non-verbal communication such as posture, facial expressions and tone of voice.

Children with ASD may experience problems in relation to play to varying degrees – in particular, imaginative play which is an important element of social development in children. Some children may also engage in repetitive behaviours, including within play, which impact upon their social interaction (Honey et al., 2006; Lam et al., 2008; Zandt et al., 2007).

For practitioners working with young children who have concerns regarding a child's communication and a possible diagnosis of ASD, there are a number of indicators that can be considered. If there are any concerns about a child's communication, it is important that the child and family are referred to the family health visitor and GP to ensure that they are promptly assessed and strategies put in place to maximise the child's potential. Indeed, the 'Autistic Spectrum Disorder exemplar' developed for the Every Child Matters National Service Framework for Children, Young People and Maternity Services (DfES and DoH, 2004) is a very useful resource for practitioners, particularly those who do not work with children with autistic spectrum disorder on a regular basis. It provides information regarding sources of help for children and families prior to diagnosis and post-diagnosis, and ongoing support from the statutory agencies. Practitioners working with children in whatever sector do need to have a good general knowledge of what autistic spectrum disorder is, as the later the signs and symptoms are actually identified and a diagnosis of ASD made, the more entrenched some repetitive behaviours – spinning fabrics/objects, rocking and finger flapping – can become.

Indicators that a child may have a form of ASD

Identifying ASD is always difficult because children are different and each child will demonstrate problems to varying degrees. It is important to have a sound knowledge of child development in order to establish what is developmentally appropriate communication and play by the child and what may indicate some difficulties. Communication is the key area to observe, particularly the social aspects, interaction with others and imagination.

From a general communication perspective, the child often does not comprehend the non-verbal signals used by peers and significant others. As well as echolalia (repeating what is said to them), the child may not respond to their name and may experience speech regression. The early social communication used by infants such as social smiles, waving goodbye or pointing is often not evident in a child with ASD. Eye contact can be particularly difficult for some children with ASD.

In terms of imagination, the child may tend to focus on play activities which are limited in range, repetitive and involve the use of patterns (lining objects up in a specific order over and over again). The child will often become upset if someone tries to change their usual play routines. The child will engage in solitary play and have difficulty in relation to associative and cooperative play.

In relation to echolalia, it can be difficult to differentiate whether the child is actually stating what they want or merely repeating the question; for example, a parent asks 'What would you like to drink' and the child with severe ASD replies 'you like to drink'. Sometimes the child may repeat certain phrases, such as those commonly used in a particular cartoon. This may again be just repetition; however, practitioners and parents/carers need to look at the context, relevance and meaning in which the phrase has been used before deciding that it demonstrates echolalia.

The National Autistic Society (NAS, 2003, p. 1) use a memorable acronym – SPELL – to aid working with children with ASD; it is often integrated into the educational setting (Tut et al., 2006) and is easy to use.

- **S**tructure – ensure that all aspects of the day are structured so the child is able to feel in control and that the events are as predictable as they can be (timetables including home and school elements can be very helpful). Any changes must be clearly communicated as far in advance as possible and reinforced regularly.

- **P**ositive – ensure that wherever possible the child's everyday experiences are positive. Build upon their potential by praising every communication, no matter how small.

- **E**mpathy – try to see the world from the child's perspective, one who struggles with sensory overload and the multiple communication demands experienced in everyday life.

- **L**ow arousal – be mindful of sensory overload experienced in the child's surroundings. Usually people are able to 'zone out' external noises and distractions in a room, but a child/young person with ASD may struggle with them, which will affect their communication with others.

- **L**inks – build on the child/young person's strengths and areas of interest so that new experiences may slowly be introduced. The links between familiar and new activities must be clearly communicated to the child/young person.

Given the particular difficulties that children and young people with ASD encounter with regards to communicating their needs, wishes and feelings (and one would argue that parents/carers/professionals may have with their own communication in relation to recognising and understanding the child's communication efforts at times), it is good to reflect upon current strategies developed to enhance communication, particularly in relation to social communication. One approach used is based on an evolved understanding of children with ASD in that a number of children and young people with ASD have a fascination and indeed preoccupation with vehicles, particularly trains (they are predictable – for example they go on set routes using track and so there is no variation, unless planned, onto more tracks; each train often does a set task (freight or passenger); each class of trains can be easily recognized; people working on trains do specific roles). Indeed it has been identified in a study involving parents of children with ASD by the NAS (2002) that this is evident in play and the particular popularity of toys such as the series of Thomas the Tank Engine and Friends™ toys and accessories not only are the qualities of trains as cited above (including the technical accuracy of the models) there are additional elements that can be useful to expand upon within social play.

ACTIVITY *4.1*

Using the SPELL (NAS, 2003) acronym think about why Thomas the Tank Engine™ toys (trains and figures), accessories, books and DVDs may be so popular amongst children with ASD.

S

P

E

L

L

Comment

Activity 4.1 can assist the reader's understanding of some of the key concepts in communication with children and young people with ASD and may enable the reader to consider using the SPELL tool to evaluate current activities undertaken with a particular child. It may also assist the reader in adapting aspects of situations that are unpredictable, for example the child needing medical attention for an injury, to enable the child to feel secure and supported.

A more recent development has been the excellent Transporters ™ animation series. It was evaluated for the NAS by the Autism Research Centre (Baron-Cohen et al., 2007) and was demonstrated as being very effective for children aged four to eight years old. The transporters are vehicles that perform predictable tasks and follow predictable patterns of movement, for example on tracks or lines. However, in contrast to the Thomas the Tank Engine™ characters, the facial features move and are based on people's expressions. Facial features are different for each character and expressions change, e.g. from a smile to a frown. These changes can be clearly seen by the child and are expected in response to a given situation in the storyline. Guidance is provided for practitioners on how to utilise the animated material alongside appropriate structured discussions with the child in relation to emotions and the interactions of others to set situations. There is a wealth of information on the Transporters TV™ website.

An ongoing project that one could argue reflects the NAS (2003) SPELL approach, is that of Gomez de la Cuesta et al. (2009) from the Autism Research Centre. They are currently evaluating the way in which children with ASD play with LEGO ™ and also whether it can be used in a more structured therapeutic way to help develop a child with ASD's social and communication skills.

To summarise this section, what is clear is that communication is always possible; only in the mind of the reader are limitations placed on it. The theme of this book is every child matters. This chapter takes it further: every disabled child matters too (Every Disabled Child Matters, 2007).

C H A P T E R   S U M M A R Y

Communication is more than words or actions; it is also about feelings, needs and wishes. A child/young person's ability to communicate these and the problems that can arise if they are not acknowledged requires that practitioners have a sound understanding of child development, family functioning and the factors that impact upon emotional intelligence and resilience. This is equally true of communication and the needs of children with disabilities. They may face barriers to communication in the form of sensory impairment or in relation to social exclusion, attitudes and assumptions regarding the needs, feelings and wishes of children with disabilities by others. Every child really does matter.

FURTHER READING

Carr A (2006) *The handbook of child and adolescent clinical psychology. A contextual approach.* London: Routledge.

This book encourages the reader to look upon the child /young person and their family and the influences parenting and professionals have too, in relation to child and adolescent mental health.

Cassidy J, Shaver PR (2008) *Handbook of attachment. Theory, research and clinical applications.* London: Guildford Press.

This book helps the reader understand the importance of attachment in more depth.

Department of Children, Schools and Families DCSF (2007) *Common assessment framework: A practitioner's guide.* London: DCSF.

Readers need a sound understanding of this when working with children and young people.

Department of Education and Skills, Department of Health (2004) *National Service Framework for children, young people and maternity services. Autistic spectrum disorders.* London: Department of Health.

Offers clear guidance regarding support that should be in place for children with ASD.

Goleman D (2005) *Emotional intelligence.* London: Bantam. 10th anniversary ed.

This book is easy to read and follow and explains the basis of current work in relation to emotional intelligence and emotional resilience.

Royal National Institute for the Deaf (RNID) (2007) *Starting to sign.* 4th edition London: RNID.

Useful if the reader wants to know more about using BSL.

Scope (2009) *Supporting communication through AAC.* London: Scope. www.scope.org.uk/education/aac

This online resource helps the reader understand how they can work with children and young people who use augmentative and alternative communication.

Chapter 5

Engaging with children, young people, families and carers at home and in other settings

Angela Shaw

Objectives

By the end of this chapter, you should have an understanding of:

- The challenges involved in engagement and communication in families and homes.

- The range of different settings in which children and young people may find themselves, particularly those who are looked after other than at home.

- The particular challenges in communicating with looked-after children and their families and carers.

- Issues of attachment and the effects on communication.

- The impact on children, young people and families when changes in the home environment occur and how this can affect communication and engagement.

- Strategies for maximising effective communication and engagement for those involved in caring for and building resilience in those receiving care.

Introduction

This chapter addresses the issues which arise when we are dealing with children, young people and families in a range of diverse settings, ranging from the family home to institutional care, hospital, foster home or school. The Common Core of Skills and Knowledge for the Children's Workforce demands that workers should be able to 'Communicate effectively with all children, young people, families and carers' (DfES, 2005b). Implicit within this statement is the assumption that the communication strategies 'within' families and 'between' children and their carers are not issues in themselves. In reality, communication with children at home, with carers at home, between children and carers and/or with any of these individuals and groups in a wider range of settings is more problematic. The setting, in itself, can affect the ways in which different professionals encounter and strive to overcome barriers to effective communication. When we incorporate into this network of complex communication difficulties the added pressure of working inter-professionally, the need to be aware of the impact of the environment becomes even more significant. Highly publicised cases, from those of Victoria Climbié in 2001 to Baby P in 2008, have highlighted that different agency workers failed consistently to communicate with each other but also with the families concerned. In the case of Baby P, it was communication with the child's birth family which failed to spot the danger; in that of Victoria Climbié, the communication failed in a case where the child was undergoing kinship care. In both cases, a range of professionals from different agencies needed to be more aware of how the environment affected the communication, as well as how their pooled knowledge could have created a different outcome.

ACTIVITY 5.1

On a blank sheet of paper, write down the three earliest conversations that you can remember having. The exact words aren't important, just a general sense of the ideas that you remember being expressed.

When you have completed the list, answer the following questions:

- *Who was the conversation with?*

- *What was the gist of the conversation? Were you in trouble? Were you being praised/ punished/informed?*

- *Why do you think that you have remembered these conversations in particular?*

Comment

As you answer the questions, you will begin to get a sense of the significance of certain communications with children. It is likely that the conversations were held with people who were very significant to you in your childhood or who were perceived to be threatening to you at the time. It is also likely that at least one of the conversations relates to a time when you were in trouble for a misdemeanour (we tend to remember communications that we found disturbing for longer than those which rewarded us). For some people, the memories will be very painful – recalling abuse or mistreatment; for others, they will bring back a sense of injustice, perhaps an occasion when you were punished for something which you had not realised was forbidden. For everyone, the activity will give you an insight to the power of interpersonal communication with young children and the resilience of the memories that communication holds.

Communicating in the home

For most children, their first experiences of interpersonal communication begin in the home with their families. For some parents, this is a spontaneous development; they move seamlessly from talking to their baby as if the child was fully aware of the words 'Aren't you a good girl?', 'Who's a beautiful boy?', 'What a lovely smile!' to having increasingly meaningful conversations as the child's own vocabulary develops. Research from Edinburgh University since the 1970s (Trevarthen and Aitken, 2003) has shown that these very early 'baby conversations' are a critical element in the child's ability to develop good communication skills in later life and later work has consolidated this evidence. Likewise, a study of 21 babies over a period of time (Markus et al., 2000) found that their language development was largely predicated on the frequency, quality and responsiveness of these early episodes of attention and communication.

For most parents/carers, these communication episodes happen entirely spontaneously. For others, however, communications such as these rarely occur and the children mature with little access to meaningful conversation throughout their childhood. For those who are working with children and families and carers in the home, this should provide a first step: listen to the adults talking to the children; assess the nature of the conversation; establish an idea of the patterns of communication in the home – are children only addressed when they misbehave? Are they asked to contribute to conversations or told to be quiet? Does the carer make eye contact with the child? Is the child addressed directly or only spoken about in the third person? By assessing these interactions, childcare workers can begin to get a sense of how the child is engaging with their carers and how they are engaging with the child. This is a critical first step in establishing good communication with each party and in establishing a rapport which will allow meaningful engagement to develop. Power is a key factor whenever professionals are working with families and one strategy for equalising the power base in engaging with children and families is to use the home environment wherein the carers and children feel that they own the physical space so are less aware of the 'threat' from professional intervention.

Even within the family home, communication and engagement are doubly difficult when the family is from a different background to the childcare worker, either in terms of race or social class. Norms which exist in one culture or group may not be reflected in another and it is difficult to differentiate where a difference is cultural, a reflection of a genuine cause for concern or simply poor communication. This was highlighted in the response to the Climbié case (Laming Report, 2003) wherein different agency workers made assumptions that racial and ethnic differences were apparent, when, in fact, this was not the case and other more sinister forces were at work. In the report, Lord Laming says:

> *Several times during this Inquiry I found myself wondering whether a failure by a particular professional to take action to protect Victoria, may have been partly due to that professional losing sight of the fact that her needs were the same as those of any other seven-year-old girl, from whatever cultural background.*
>
> (Para. 16.2)

In the field, those who work with children and families, when faced with problems, must make a judgement based on training, knowledge and experience, and underpinned by two critical factors – good, effective communication and the ability to share information with colleagues across all relevant agencies.

Communicating outside the family home

If assessing and using communication effectively with children and families in their own homes is both complex and challenging, then it becomes even more problematic when the setting is other than the home. In these cases, the power-base shifts away from the child or parent/carer and into the hands of the professional before the communication even begins. Thus parents who are quite confident in their own homes will become reticent or aggressive when in a day care setting, school, hospital or family centre. Childcare workers need to look at ways to equalise the power-base in order to ensure that children and carers are empowered to communicate effectively. This can be done primarily with adult parents/carers through good communication strategies, by listening actively to them, inviting their opinions and treating their input with respect. Similar strategies can also be employed with children who may well feel doubly disempowered; on the one hand, because the other communicator is an adult and, on the other, because the physical environment is not their home territory. With these children, it is critical to employ some straightforward strategies to enhance the sense of respect. These include:

- Not using terms of endearment rather than their given name.

- Not making physical gestures such as hugging them.

- Ensuring that eye contact is made easily by sitting at the child's level.

- Listening carefully to their input and responding in such a way that they know they are being heard – for example, by reflecting back their last statement to check that you have understood.

These strategies are not just useful ones to bear in mind for communicating with children in difficult situations but are also good practice for any meaningful interpersonal interaction, whatever the setting or circumstances. Nevertheless, they are particularly significant when a child is especially vulnerable through being in an unfamiliar setting.

For many children, their first experience of being in a setting other than at home comes when they enter nursery or school. This is now an almost universal experience for everyone living in Britain and so it is easy to forget that for thousands of years until relatively recently it would have been very strange indeed to have a situation where children were not in the same physical environment as their close family. Indeed, within the last two generations, the situation wherein children are spending large amounts of time away from their families has changed. The advent of a society in which many families have two parents out at work and the children are in some form of day care has only become the norm since the 1970s and has led to some interesting debate and research about the effects of such separation (England, 1996).

Throughout the last 500 years a division relating to social class in relation to children being separated from their parents and families has always existed. In times past, children from upper-class backgrounds would often be removed from their birth mother and taken to a wet nurse; they would only return to the family home when they were old enough to behave in an acceptable manner in adult company (Fildes, 1988). In a similar vein, the male children of the upper classes would be sent away to boarding school from a very early age to enjoy an expensive education (Leinster-Mackay, 1984). Despite these instances, the vast majority of children in the days before universal statutory education would spend their lives in the company of their immediate family for all or most of the time. Even in modern Britain, the majority of children will spend most of their time with their families despite the rise in time spent in day care and school, but if we examine the number of *waking hours* that children spend with their families, this percentage decreases. Ironically, older children will spend more waking hours with their families than the youngest children, simply because they will require fewer hours sleep.

ACTIVITY 5.2

Think back to your first day at nursery or school. Was it a good experience? Can you remember how you felt? Were you excited or afraid? Did it live up to your expectations/fears? If so, how did it do so? If not, why not?

Imagine you are preparing a three-year-old child for their first day at nursery or school. Using your own experience as a guide, write down the three key things that you would say to the child.

As you look back on what you have written, reflect on whether you have picked three things that could apply to all children in this situation or whether they only reflect your personal experience. If possible, discuss what you have written with other people doing the same exercise. How do your answers differ? Has one person assumed that the child will be excited and another assumed that they will be distressed? How can you know which approach to take in preparing a child for their first day away from home alone?

Comment

You may have decided that it is best to assume that the child will be distressed and to prepare for that eventuality, or to talk to the child about their fears/hopes/expectations before setting a preparation plan. You may have decided to liaise with nursery/school staff in advance, or that you are best placed to make the decisions alone. There is no 'right' answer, but giving thought and care to the preparation can effect the transfer much more smoothly.

Although starting nursery or school provides many children with their earliest separation from the family home, for many children in present-day Britain, day care outside the home begins at a much earlier stage and preparation via verbal communication is not possible. In 1980, the Oxford Pre-school Research Project (Bruner, 1980) produced a report which suggested that the quality of day care in Britain left much to be desired and that the children who were routinely left for many hours with childminders or other caregivers could suffer long-term damage, partly because the level of interaction and communication was less than they would receive from their birth mother. In the years that have followed, more rigorous research has examined the same set of issues, notably the National Institute of

Child Health and Human Development Research Project (Clarke-Stewart, 1998). These later studies are less damning than the Bruner study but have come to some similar conclusions. It seems, then, that for every child's development to really matter, we need to make sure that high quality communication, engagement and interpersonal interaction is inbuilt into all their lives and this places a particular responsibility on those who work with children outside the family home.

If some children in modern Britain spend a relatively small number of hours interacting in the family home, for others the family home is no longer their place of residence and contact with their birth family can be very restricted or completely absent. This situation poses substantial challenges to childcare workers; communication and engagement with children, families and carers when the children are in settings outside the family home, whether at school, in day care or in a residential setting, involves particular problems and responsibilities. It also presents additional challenges in engaging with the 'different' forms of carer, from those who are providing kinship care to those providing foster care, day care or educational support.

Children's diverse home circumstances

For the majority of children in Britain in the twenty-first century, their home is where their parent/s, siblings and close family members are living. For other children, 'home' can have a different meaning. For some, it is the home of extended family members, such as grand-parents, aunts and uncles, or other kin. For others, home is a temporary foster home, perhaps with foster carers whom they have known before or with complete strangers. For a number of children, home is an institutional setting. It is in this respect that definitions of 'home' can become difficult. Some children can spend years in hospital or months in boarding school, much longer than other children spend in foster care or a residential home, yet the hospital or boarding school will never be classified as home to them or their families. This is significant when we are examining the whole issue of engagement, both with the children and with their families or carers, as the internalised classification of the setting to these people affects their sense of power, or powerlessness, within it. In a hospital the child and their family or carers will never feel a sense of ownership of the space occupied that they might be expected to feel in a foster or residential home. As a consequence, they will always feel disempowered in the relationships which exist in that setting. The key issue for workers is to examine honestly where the balance of power lies in the setting and tailor the communication and engagement strategies to maximise the ownership of the environment for the child and their family and carers. Failure to acknowledge the balance of power damages the communication from the outset and can serve to further undermine the child's resilience, and increase the parents' and carers' anxieties and sense of isolation. This is also true of educational settings, and parents will often report their anxiety when they attend 'parent–teacher evenings' and are told how difficult their child is. The parents themselves may well recognise these difficulties but are able to do so from the cocoon of an emotional bond which is not shared by the teacher. Teachers frequently bemoan the fact that parents do not support their efforts to discipline children in school (Ofsted, 1999), yet fail to realise that they inevitably alienate the same parents and force them to take sides with their children because they too feel under attack from the teachers.

Schools, hospitals and day care establishments are therefore not classified by the children themselves as *home*, even if they spend the majority of their time in these establishments. The Oxford Pre-school Research Project also suggested that this was true of very young children in the care of childminders, despite the commonly held belief that this form of provision would give an alternative home-from-home.

For children in institutional care or long-term foster care, the situation can be even more complex. Technically, if they are resident in the setting, that is their home. For many, however, there is another (more potent) home environment elsewhere – the place where their parents, siblings or other kin reside. Children in these settings will therefore often differentiate in their conversations between the two forms of home. Where the institutional setting or foster home is physically distanced from the family home children can feel particularly isolated and express concerns about the severance from their roots (Skuse and Ward, 2003).

CASE STUDY

Jon is nine years old. He has had a difficult time for the last three years since his new step-father, James, moved into the family home. Prior to James moving in, Jon shared the family home with his mother, who was a lone parent and in the last three years he has continued to live there but now also has two younger siblings, aged one and two. Jon's mother, Maria, has a problem with drug misuse and met James when she was searching for a supplier. Prior to James moving in, Jon spent a lot of time with his grandparents but they didn't like James so all contact ceased about two years ago. Since then Jon's attendance at school has been sporadic and his behaviour (as observed by neighbours) has become increasingly anti-social. Last week Jon scratched James' van with his bicycle and James told Maria that she has to choose between the two of them. She has agreed to his demands and has asked social services if they will place Jon in care and see if he can be placed for adoption.

You are asked to talk at length to Jon to find out what he wants to do and to look at ways that you can support him in ensuring the best outcome for him, his mother, his siblings and the family as a whole. Make a list of what strategies you will employ to ensure that Jon feels safe and empowered to confide in you with his needs. Write down what possible outcomes you can suggest for Jon, which other professionals you will need to talk to about his situation and which family members you need to engage with. Make an outline plan of who you will talk to, when you will talk to them and what strategies you need to employ to ensure that everyone feels comfortable with your engagement. Finally, reflect upon and make a list of your value judgements relating to Jon, his mother and his step-father. What personal values could have an impact on your engagement with each of them? What effect would the revelation of these values have on the effectiveness of the engagement? How can you ensure that your own beliefs and values don't colour your judgement as to the best outcome for all the people concerned?

Comment

There are no correct answers to the above case study activity but the critical factor in the engagement and communication is that you need to be as sensitive to the needs of all the parties involved as possible. It is impossible, as human beings, to suppress all our attitudes, values and beliefs, but it is vital to try to ensure that we are aware of them and to attempt as far as possible to engage with others who may have different value bases in a way which allows them to be empowered and honest.

There are a range of possible outcomes for Jon, which you may have considered – foster care, adoption or residential care. You may have looked at ways to continue to support him at home or considered approaching his grandparents to see if they could/would provide foster care – a growing trend for families in crisis. For children who are fostered with family members, known as kinship care, the problems inherent in fostering can be minimised as the interconnecting roots of their kin can form a security net. The importance and strength of kinship care is now being recognised by the government and encouraged as a means of supporting children and parents in a way that helps to preserve children's sense of identity whilst they are unable to be cared for in the parental home:

> For those children and young people who need to be cared for outside their immediate family, we should, at all relevant stages of the care planning process, explore the potential for enabling children to live with or be supported by wider family and friends.
> (DfES, 2007a, pp. 5–6)

For children who are fostered outside the kinship network, different forms of fostering apply. For some children, foster care is classified as respite care, especially where a child has serious disabilities and the parents need to have the opportunity for respite time. For others, short-term fostering is required to provide care whilst parents have temporary difficulties or health problems. Long-term or permanent foster care is usually provided for children who are unlikely to be able to return to the family home but who are not considered suitable for adoption, perhaps because of regular contact with the birth family or because of the risk of abuse. There are a number of variations within these broad categories, such as bridging care or emergency care, but the overall aim is always to provide the child with an alternative form of home which is as close to a family home setting as possible.

For some children, adoption into another family unit, distinct from their birth family, is a reality (this is not true of all adoptions, as some children are formally adopted by step-parents or other kin and thus remain within the kinship network of their birth family). For these children and their families and carers, the adoptive family becomes the 'real' family, legally and emotionally. It does, however, need to be considered in a different way when we are examining communication and engagement with families, as the existence of another kinship network in the child's past can have a profound effect on both the child and their family and carers, especially as the child reaches adolescence and may begin to question their unknown or forgotten 'other family'.

The quality of care

Other chapters of this book introduce theories relating to attachment. The work of John Bowlby (1951) in the 1950s suggested that children who were separated from their main caregiver, assumed at the time to be the mother, displayed a regular sequence of distressed behaviours. Since this idea was first raised, numerous debates have taken place questioning the validity of the original hypothesis, citing political agenda at play, counter-arguments and later experimental evidence to refute the idea (Rutter and Taylor, 1981). Despite these challenges, there remains a firm body of evidence to suggest that children need to be able to form secure attachments to a caregiver, whether mother, father or other carer, in order to thrive.

This raises the question of the quality of care and the depth and strength of attachment for children who are spending large amounts of time in settings other than at home with their birth family. If we are to communicate and engage effectively with children, families and carers in these situations, we need to be aware of the constraints afforded by the relationships' strengths or weaknesses. Where a child is distressed, the effectiveness of any engagement will be undermined but the distress itself may not be immediately apparent; indeed, with older children and adolescents, the outward demeanour can suggest that no distress is in evidence. Likewise, for those who are caring for children in residential settings or foster homes, there can be a need to appear to be attached in ways that are unrealistic but felt by the carer to be imperative to display. Recent research (Elfer et al., 2002) discusses some of these difficulties and cites the organisational constraints involved in creating meaningful engagement, such as holidays, shifts and staff changes. These sorts of issues have also led some to argue (Dahlberg et al., 1999) that childcare workers in these settings should not create 'false closeness', but instead a complex network connecting shared activities with all the people, the adults as well as the other children in the setting, and with the environment itself.

One of the critical theories to underpin the issues surrounding these relationships is provided by Carl Rogers (1961), with the notion of conditional and unconditional love. Rogers, and others in the humanistic tradition of psychology, believed that human beings need unconditional love in order to thrive and it is in this area that children in care settings can often find the distinct difference in their lives from those who are in their birth family. Essentially, conditional love says, 'I love you because you are good, pretty, clever, a source of pride. . .'; unconditional love says, 'I love you even though you are badly behaved, rude, ugly, a source of concern. . .'. Often, when there is a tragic case in the national press where some young person commits a serious crime, there is speculation about the support they continue to get from their own family. What is rarely acknowledged is that the criminal's family are usually victims too because their love for the criminal is not conditional upon them being law-abiding but has been unconditional since the day of their arrival on earth. In this respect, children who are being cared for outside their birth family can often find that herein lies the critical difference between themselves and those who are cared for within their own family of origin.

To a lesser extent, this is also to be seen in situations where care is temporary, such as day care. It was noted by the Oxford Pre-school Research Project in relation to childminders, and personal experience visiting childminder homes would support this. Frequently the minder would report that they were 'more strict with my own than with the others' but prolonged observation would reveal exactly the opposite, especially when it came to situations where children were behaving badly and then seeking reassurance that they had been forgiven. None of this is a surprise when we consider the nature and power of evolution, which demands that, in order for a species to survive, it is essential that parents and families are hard-wired to protect their young from the outside world. What is significant for those who are working to communicate and engage with children and carers outside the family home setting is the need to recognise the multiple forces at play within the child–carer relationship, the carer–childcare worker relationship and child–childcare worker relationship.

ACTIVITY **5.3**

On a sheet of paper describe a simple scenario in which a child or teenager behaves very badly towards you (it could be taking something of yours which doesn't belong to them; telling a damaging lie about you to someone else; spoiling a relationship which you value; damaging something which you hold precious to you; or any similar scenario).

Turn over the paper and write down the names of two people:

• *Someone whom you love very dearly – a child, parent, sibling or partner.*

• *Someone whom you like very much – a friend, colleague, cousin or neighbour.*

Now imagine each of the two people doing the 'bad thing' on the other side of the paper:

• *How would you feel?*

• *Would you feel differently about each of the people involved?*

• *What would be the long-term effect?*

Comment

Most people would be equally angry and upset at the outcome of the bad behaviour, no matter who had committed it. The critical difference, in most cases, would be the long-term effect. With someone whom you love unconditionally, you would find ways to rationalise the behaviour over time and the long-term effects would be minimal. For those whom you merely like very much – a much more conditional situation – the damage to the relationship in the long term would be substantial and could easily lead to complete estrangement.

Unfortunately, human beings cannot control the levels of conditional and unconditional care which they feel for others, whether those others are children or adults. To varying extents, this is a product of our evolution, a reflection of our personality and a product of our environment. What we need to recognise in our engagement with children and families, however, is that unconditional love cannot be *created* by effort of will and to pretend that it can (as in the case of the previously mentioned childminders who reiterated constantly that they felt it for their charges) is to risk assuming that children are receiving a quality of childhood experience which is, in fact, not the case. When childcare workers are forced to find places for children outside the family unit they need to be realistic in their assessment of those places and to look at a wide range of factors involved in providing high quality care that increases a child's resilience and makes them able to mature into loving adults who can then provide unconditional care for their own children. At the heart of this process is successful engagement with the children themselves, their families and carers, and significant others in the wider community. For children who are the responsibility of the state because of problems in their birth family environment and for children who are temporarily in the care of others in settings such as hospitals, schools and day care establishments, the critical issue lying at the heart of the choices which the state or the parents must make is the quality of the care provided.

For children in care, i.e. those who are in the care of the state through legislation, assessments of quality have changed immeasurably over the last 50 years. Quality of care was considered very much to be that which was reflected in tangible evidence through the 1950s and 1960s, such as a lack of poverty. Today we recognise that a child is usually better placed in their family unit, however poor that may be materially, than in a remote environment where their care can be conditional upon their behaviour. Quality of care reflects a wide range of issues but good communication and effective engagement are critical factors. For those who are part of the childcare workforce, the challenge is to listen, respond, adjust to the setting, the respondent, the situation and to provide appropriate support for all the parties involved. In all of these encounters, competence builds through practice, reflection and – crucially – by a recognition of the power-balance in every relationship: adult–child, adult–adult, childcare worker–parent/carer, parent/carer–child. The key is to remember always that:

> *Whether it involves children, babies or adults, interpersonal communication is a two way process.*
>
> (Petrie, 1997, p. 25)

Relinquishing power so that communication is truly two-way can be very challenging but is always the best way to ensure the highest quality of outcome for children, their families and carers.

C H A P T E R   S U M M A R Y

Communication and engagement with children, carers and families in their own homes or in settings other than at home pose particular challenges to childcare workers. The nature of the environment impacts on communication and engagement in a range of ways and workers need to be aware of how a particular setting can influence success or failure in connecting with others. This chapter has addressed the need to recognise issues of power which are tied to the ownership of some environments and be aware of how a setting can influence the nature of communication and engagement. It has introduced some of the key issues, relating to different settings, of which childcare workers need to be aware – including the limitations of care beyond the home, the nature of carer–child relationships, conditional and unconditional love, assessment of the quality of care within and beyond the home, and the potential for empowering or disempowering others during the processes of engagement.

Dahlberg G, Moss P and Pence AR (1999) *Beyond quality in early childhood education and care*. London and Philadelphia, PA: Falmer Press.

A book which provides a postmodern view of the key issues in communication and engagement with children, highlighting how different interpretations are introduced in attempts to describe practice.

Elfer, P, Goldschmeid, E and Selleck, D (2002) *Key persons in nurseries: Building relationships for quality provision*. London: NEYN.

This book examines the different roles of people engaged with very young children and provides a range of perspectives relating to their influence.

Foley P, Roche J and Tucker S (2001) *Children in society: Contemporary theory, policy and practice*. Basingstoke: Open University Press/Palgrave.

This is a general text which can provide a wealth of material for anyone working with children and families. It covers all aspects of engagement as well as communication and has excellent chapters relating to resilience and quality of life.

Petrie, P (1997) *Communicating with children and adults: Interpersonal skills for early years and play work*. London: Edward Arnold.

This book provides practical guidance for those who wish to develop their own communication and engagement skills.

Chapter 6

Communicating with children, young people and families in health care contexts

Barbara Elliott

Objectives

By the end of this chapter, you should have an understanding of:

- Factors influencing communication with children, young people and families in health care contexts.

- Effective communication strategies to promote children's understanding of health care issues and facilitate their ability to cope with illness and treatment.

- The role of effective communication in promoting successful family functioning through diagnosis and treatment of illness in children and young people.

Introduction

Communicating with children and young people in health care contexts acknowledges their rights to be informed about and involved in health care decisions that affect them. Children need to know what is happening to them, feel able to ask questions and expect honest answers in terms they can understand. No longer is it acceptable to 'protect' children from the reality of their situation. Whether that means explaining their illness or disability to them or procedures that they must undergo, childcare professionals now approach children as active participants in, rather than passive recipients of, health care. This recognition of the rights of children to participate in and negotiate their own health care is a result of a shift in the way that health professionals and childcare workers view children. It may be seen as a consequence of the ratification of the Convention on the Rights of the Child (United Nations Convention on the Rights of the Child, 1989) and the increasing value placed on children's opinions of and participation in the development of all aspects of their lives, including education and recreation, as promoted through the *Children's Plan* (DCSF, 2007a), *Every*

Child Matters (DfES, 2003) and the *National Service Framework for Children, Young People and Maternity Services* (DoH, 2004a).

Clear and effective communication with children, young people and their families as demanded by the *Common Core of Skills and Knowledge for the Children's Workforce* (DfES, 2005) is an expectation of anyone working with children in any setting. The benefits of sound communication skills are explained elsewhere in this book, but in health care settings there are additional benefits. Effective communication in health care settings enables education about healthy lifestyle choices, health care interventions, illness or proposed treatment for both children and their families. One of the key principles of the government's strategy for children and young people's health (DoH and DCSF, 2009) is that parents receive the information they need to support their children's health. Sharing information with children and families increases involvement in decisions and results in increased cooperation and satisfaction with health care for both children and their families. Successful long-term management of chronic diseases such as diabetes and asthma relies on shared decision making and concordance based on sound patient education and facilitation of self-management (Theunissen and Tates, 2004; Vacik et al., 2001).

However, health care settings also present additional barriers to effective communication which must be considered and addressed. Two of the most common complaints of consumers of health care are lack of information and poor communication. These problems may be particularly evident when those consumers are children. Children and young people may be frightened by their illness, pain and the unfamiliar environment of hospitals and surgeries. The language and culture of health care workers may be unintelligible and make children and their families feel disadvantaged and disorientated. In spite of recent developments in children's participation in health care, they remain relatively powerless and depend on adults to provide honest information in a form that they can understand and to provide opportunities for their views to be heard (Eliott and Watson, 2000). Unfortunately, dissatisfaction with communication in health care settings has been frequently reported both by children and their parents (Ammentorp et al., 2005; Farmer et al., 2004) and there is much that can be done to improve communication with children, young people and their families in such settings.

The vast majority of health care delivery to children involves a multi-professional approach including doctors, children's nurses, social workers, dieticians, physiotherapists, health visitors, psychologists, teachers, play specialists and youth workers, as well as voluntary workers. Good communication within these teams is essential in ensuring delivery of high quality care.

This chapter explores a number of key issues in communication in health care settings and enables readers to develop their knowledge and skills in this area. A number of activities provide the reader with opportunities to explore their current knowledge and skills regarding communication and reflect on their ability to adapt these to health care settings. Suggestions for making communication with children successful and ensuring encounters in health care settings are 'child friendly' have been provided and further reading is suggested at the end of this chapter for those wishing to develop their knowledge further.

Children's understanding of health

Effective communication with children has to recognise their unique understanding of health and illness which will vary with age, educational level, experience and culture. Drawings by six- and seven-year-old children suggest that they associate health with being young and sporty and illness with old age, needing a walking stick and pools of vomit (Hooton, 2000). Children appreciate that illness is inside their body before they understand how external factors can cause illness (Vacik et al., 2001) but older children are aware of the many factors influencing health such as smoking, exercise and nutrition and appreciate that they can influence their own health (Hooton, 2000).

One of the key aims of communicating with children in health care settings is to reduce their anxiety. Understanding children's beliefs about health and illness will guide effective communication as childcare workers often have to start explanations by dispelling some of the myths that children hold about health and hospitals. For example, children frequently believe that they are to blame for their illness, seeing it as punishment for some misdemeanour. Some families use hospital as a threat with children in an effort to get them to adopt healthy behaviours such as eating healthily and avoiding dangerous play areas. Experience of relatives being ill and in hospital can increase children's understanding but may also add to their fear and misunderstanding (McGrath and Huff, 2001). Television programmes do not give children realistic impressions of what happens when people are ill and in hospital but they do give insights and can be a useful starting point for discussions with them. Explanations that acknowledge children's understanding of health and illness and begin by asking children what they expect from their illness or encounter in a health care setting are more likely to be effective. It is clear that, where children do not have accurate information, they fill the gaps in their knowledge with imagination and their imagined realities can be far more frightening than their genuine situation.

Cultural issues not only influence children's understanding of health but also the methods and effectiveness of communication in health care settings. Culture does not simply relate to a child's religion, ethnic origin or place of birth but is a term used to define 'the norms of behaviour and shared values among a particular group of people' (Masters, 2005, p. 157). Professionals working in health care settings need to develop cultural competence; that is, behaviours and attitudes which are embedded into the practice methods of the workplace and its professionals that enable them to work effectively in cross-cultural situations (Arnold, 2007). Personal cultural beliefs influence how the behaviour of others is interpreted and how individuals respond to them and awareness of these beliefs is the first step in developing cultural competence.

In health care settings communication is influenced by issues such as locus of control, social class and education, as well as the personal cultural beliefs of the individuals involved. Health care professionals can appear far removed from the young people they are trying to help because they have both adult and institutional authority and their cultural beliefs are influenced by their professional values as well as their personal experiences and background. Understanding where these beliefs originate enables health care workers to be more self-aware and appreciate the cultural differences between themselves and their young clients. It is essential that young people see health care workers as non-judgemental and feel able to confide in them and turn to them for help. The following activity will help to identify the cultural influences on your beliefs about teenage pregnancy and how these beliefs can have an impact on effective communication.

ACTIVITY **6.1**

Think about your opinion of teenage pregnancy. Consider what has influenced your opinion – is it religious beliefs, personal or family experiences, friends, media, politics? Write a list of all the positive and negative factors associated with teenage pregnancy and note where your understanding of those factors has come from. Discuss your beliefs with a friend and compare your understanding of and approach to teenage pregnancy.

How do you think your personal opinions might influence your communication with a young girl who confides in you that she is pregnant? Write down your possible inter-pretations of her behaviour and how these might influence your behaviour towards her.

Comment

This activity will have highlighted your personal views and attitudes towards one specific health issue. You could repeat it regarding other issues, such as drug abuse, smoking or obesity, to explore your own personal cultural beliefs. It is likely that your beliefs vary slightly to those of your friend but your understanding of yourself and each other will have increased. This is an important basis from which to develop sensitive and open communication skills.

In the UK, childcare and health professionals come from a range of cultures, although some groups are more represented in certain professions than others. The children they care for come from a wide range of cultures also. A child's culture may be defined by their family background and where they live but, as the child grows older, other factors influence the social groups to which they belong such as their choice of clothes, music and hobbies. Certain cultures are associated with adolescence and the media portrayal of teenagers and specific issues such as 'binge drinking' and 'gang culture' can create a negative image of this age group, which subsequently influences their care. Young people have reported feeling uncomfortable and unwanted in health care settings and that once they were no longer viewed as cute and worthy of sympathy when ill, health care professionals had negative images of them; they felt that doctors did not believe them, dismissing or trivialising their complaints (Eliott and Watson, 2000). Young people develop words and methods of communication that may be different to adults and younger children and health care professionals need to be aware of the different meanings assigned to certain words such as 'sick', 'wicked' and 'cool', as well as preferred methods of communication. For example, looking at an information website with a young person or discussing appropriate social networking groups may be a useful way of initiating and developing communication pathways. A study of recently diagnosed adults with rheumatoid disease found that online activities were frequent, and greater satisfaction with medical encounters was reported if this internet information was discussed with the doctor (Hay et al., 2008). Similarly, Thon and Ullrich (2008) found that the internet was an important source of information for parents of children with rheumatic disease.

Intercultural communication takes place between persons or groups from different cultures and can be particularly challenging in health care settings where the different professional groups use their own language and abbreviations, which are difficult for other professionals to understand let alone the parents or children involved. Professionals working with children in such settings often have to interpret and explain information to parents and children in terminology that is meaningful to them. Children have suggested that doctors use over-complicated language and jargon when speaking to them about health issues (Eliott and Watson, 2000). In a small study of parents of children with disabilities, Koshti-Richman (2008) found that parents commented on how their interactions with health service personnel improved once they became familiar with the jargon they used.

Access to and involvement in health care

In ensuring that health care settings are accessible to all children and young people, it is essential that those working in them have good communication skills and can make the children and young people feel welcome and valued. Young children are reliant on their parents for access to health care and most of the communication regarding health issues is through their parents. As children grow older, schools are often used as health care settings for immunisation sessions and health promotion. School nurses may provide regular drop-in clinics in schools and increasingly provide sexual health services there. However, outside school, young people may be unaware of what health services are available and how to access them. Surveys of children and young people have found problems with the way health care professionals communicate with them and young people often feel intimidated and too frightened to ask certain questions. If children and young people are to benefit from health services, the health promotion messages must be delivered at an appropriate level and be sensitive to their needs. Young people need to be listened to, understood, respected and supported instead of being patronised and blamed for their situation (Chambers, 2007).

A study of over 200 children aged 4–16 found that children had a number of concerns about communication in both primary (such as GP practices) and secondary (such as hospitals) health care settings (Eliott and Watson, 2000). Doctors in particular were criticised by the young people for automatically talking to their parents or other adults rather than to them. Children of all ages felt annoyed and upset if they were completely excluded from discussions about their health and older young people found it embarrassing as well:

If you're sat there with your mum and there's something wrong with you, they just stand there talking to your mum instead of you. You're just sat there like a dummy in a chair.

(Young person aged 15; ibid., p. 115)

Other studies of children's encounters with GPs have found similar problems, with children being excluded from the interview and only rarely being given information about diagnosis and treatment directly (Tates et al., 2002). Nurses have also been found to interact with caregivers (usually mothers) rather than the children and young people who are their patients (Baggens, 2001). Research in the US found that nurses spent only 39.75 minutes interacting with their child patients during an eight-hour shift and that nurse–child interactions lasted an average of 4.24 minutes and occurred mainly during direct nursing care activities (Shin and White-Traut, 2005). Although nurses initiated interactions and encouraged them to participate, the children did not actively present their interests or introduce topics into the conversations (ibid.).

The Children and Young People's Unit developed core principles for the participation of children and young people and these underpinned the *National Service Framework for Children, Young People and Maternity Services* (DoH, 2004a). Children's participation in the planning and development of services is crucial if these services are to meet their needs and this is now recognised by all key agencies involved in children's health (DoH, 2003, 2009; Royal College of Paediatrics and Child Health, 2009).

Skills to enable health care practitioners to present a child friendly service have been explored and Chambers (2005) presents a list of dos and don'ts for those working with children in primary care settings. She suggests that the following strategies are useful in order to appear child friendly:

- Acknowledge and greet the child or young person.
- Talk to the parents or carers first to give the child time and space to relax.
- Smile or look sad as appropriate.
- Maintain good eye contact with the child.
- Observe, wait and listen. Careful observation and attentive listening can provide valuable information and improve cooperation.
- Be calm to show you are in control.
- Give simple and clear information.
- Take time; do not hurry.
- Communicate at an age-appropriate level.
- Demonstrate on a doll what you expect the child to do.
- Give the child choice wherever possible to enable them to maintain some control.
- Play; try to make the encounter fun for the child.
- Distract the child or young person by talking to them about school, hobbies, etc.
- Acknowledge their feelings and efforts to communicate.
- Give enthusiastic praise to the child.
- Reward their cooperation and acknowledge their efforts with items such as stickers and bravery certificates.

People working with children should not:

- Stand over the child.
- Use force.
- Promise things that cannot be delivered.

- Express frustration or blame, or criticise the child or young person.

- Expect the same level of understanding and cooperation of children of different ages.

- Ask too many questions.

   (adapted from Chambers, 2005, p. 16)

Confidentiality is an important issue for young people accessing primary health care services. There is evidence to suggest that teenagers' concerns relating to embarrassment and confidentiality influence consultation rates about sensitive topics (Churchill and McPherson, 2005). For example, Churchill et al. (2000) found that teenage conception rates were linked to the age, gender and skill mix of health care professionals in general practices.

Different childcare professionals have different professional codes of conduct regarding confidentiality and it is important that young people know that in health care settings their rights to privacy and confidentiality will be respected, if at all possible. There will be situations when child protection issues mean that others have to be informed of a young person's situation in order to protect them from harm but, in general, young people can be reassured that consultations with health professionals are confidential. Childcare workers employed in health care settings need to be aware of and adhere to specific practice policies regarding confidentiality.

CASE STUDY

Jane is a nursery nurse employed in her local health centre. As she is walking through the waiting room at the end of a baby clinic, she sees her friend's brother, James. She is delighted and says hello but he seems embarrassed when he sees her and looks away. The next time she is at her friend's house she challenges James about this and says, 'You were pretty grumpy when I saw you at the doctors'; were you very poorly?'

- *How has Jane broken patient confidentiality?*

- *What do you think the impact might be on James' inclination to return to the health centre?*

Comment

This activity demonstrates how Jane's innocent delight at seeing James could have a huge impact on his confidence in the security and confidentiality of health care services. Fear of being recognised and challenged about their reason for attending health care settings can make young people reluctant to access the services available to them. All staff must be made aware of the need to protect the privacy of young people, and of their duty regarding confidentiality.

The Confidentiality Toolkit (Royal College of General Practitioners and Brook, 2000) is a training pack clearly explaining the issues of confidentiality for teenagers and providing sample statements and policies. Communicating information with other services is key to good health care but there will always be concern about issues of confidentiality. There is a

Code of Practice regarding confidentality in the NHS (DOH, 2003) and a range of documents to guide staff in issues of confidentiality when sharing information about patients with other agencies, including voluntary agencies (www.dh.gov.uk).

Communication with children who are sick and/or in pain

Children who are anxious and frightened due to pain and illness may find it difficult to communicate their feelings and fears, particularly to strangers. Children are particularly vulnerable during illness and hospitalisation and verbal communication is often inadequate for young children as they are unable to comprehend beyond what their senses tell them (Baggens, 2001). James (1998) suggests that illness represents a condensed symbol of childhood, as the experiences of dependency and vulnerability are intensified. Illness also affects the child's relationships within the family and with their peers and friends. Children who were once confident and outgoing, developing independence from their parents, may become withdrawn and dependent whilst ill. Regression in developmental milestones is common during illness and for some time after recovery. Understanding of normal development of communication skills in children and young people, discussed elsewhere in this book, is essential but childcare workers must also understand the impact of illness and hospitalisation on these skills. The challenge for childcare workers is to reach out to children who are sick and connect with them at a time when they least feel like making new friends or communicating effectively.

ACTIVITY 6.2

Consider how you might show respect for and interest in children of different ages: pre-school (0–4 years), school age (5–10 years), young adolescent (11–14 years) and late adolescent (15–18 years).

- *Think of the activities and interests of the different age groups and how these could be adapted if the child or young person is ill.*

- *Consider how these normal activities could help in communication and assist the child to develop coping skills.*

- *Think of the non-verbal communication skills you might use with different age groups, such as stroking and rocking young children, facial expression and body posture with older children.*

- *Consider how you might use skills such as humour and active listening to communicate.*

Comment

As you work through this activity you will see how knowledge of activities with children and young people who are healthy can be adapted for situations when they are unwell. For example, children who enjoy being physically active with whom you might play ball games in a nursery may enjoy patting a balloon or blowing bubbles whilst they are less mobile and requiring rest. Finding activities that they can enjoy and which bring a sense of normality to their situation communicates to children that staff are interested in and care about them. Such activities also bring a sense of achievement and fun, as well as comfort and distraction from the potential pain and distress of their condition. Laughter may not be the only medicine and humour is not appropriate in all situations, but children often have a great sense of humour even in adversity and helping them to laugh and have fun is therapeutic for all concerned. Children enjoy silly rhymes and appreciate staff who are happy and can share a joke when appropriate. At other times, sensitive non-verbal communication is essential in conveying support and care for children who are ill.

Play is often used to help children express their emotions, as they often find it easier to communicate powerful feelings by transferring them to characters in a picture or story. Health care professionals often use play as a means of communicating with children and gaining their trust and cooperation. Children feel more secure and are more likely to trust adults who play with them and show interest in them as well as their illness or condition (Haiait et al., 2003). Even adolescents respond better to staff who show an interest in them by discussing hobbies, favourite sports teams or music.

Children at different ages require different approaches to communication but all children require kindness and understanding when they are sick. Babies and toddlers respond well to soothing voices, gentle stroking and rocking. Familiar lullabies and music can reduce anxiety and it is important to encourage parents to continue to communicate with their child in familiar ways even if they are very sick or even unconscious. Hearing is the last of the senses to be lost and the first to return (Sisson, 1990), so very sick children still require the soothing gentle sound of a human voice, and storytelling and nursery rhymes are an important link with normality. Preschool children respond well to play and storytelling as a means of communication and through the school years children may become increasingly involved in decision making about their health care. For example, they may be able to choose between taking medication in tablet or liquid form, which may help them to feel more in control and able to influence their care.

Research studies that have evaluated children's experiences of communication in health care contexts have found both positive and negative aspects of the encounters. Children's encounters with doctors have been the focus of a number of studies, although their views on a range of health care services have also been sought. A recent focus has been on children's voices and choices in health care services and how choice for children and young people can be promoted (Coad and Houston, 2007; Coad and Shaw, 2008). Studies of adult patient recollection of critical illness and intensive care experiences report disturbing accounts of inability to communicate, hallucinations, pain, anxiety and memory of distressing procedures (Granberg et al., 1996). Research with children recovering from critical illness is sadly lacking but there is some evidence which suggests that 15 per cent of children aged 4–16 years had negative experiences, including lack of sleep, pain, thirst and fear (Playfor et al., 2000). Noyes (2000) studied the experiences of young ventilator-dependent people in hospital and found that they were unable to communicate their needs and views effectively to the multidisciplinary team and were thus treated as passive recipients of health care rather than active participants. The inability of children and young people to adequately communicate their needs whilst ill and in hospital requires further investigation and development of improved strategies for communicating with children who are critically ill.

Preparation for hospitalisation and procedures

Effective communication and information giving is crucial in preparing children for hospitalisation and procedures in order to facilitate informed decision making and reduce anxiety. Informed consent cannot be obtained unless the child and parents fully understand the proposed treatment and this understanding cannot be achieved without effective communication. However, the importance of effective preparation of children and parents is not simply to gain their agreement to and cooperation with treatment but also to help them anticipate and cope with the events they will experience.

Evidence has been available since the 1970s that children who are given appropriate psychological preparation cope better with admission to hospital and procedures, demonstrating less anxiety and maladaptive behaviours, requiring less medication and recovering quicker (Azarnoff, 1976; Wolfer and Visintainer, 1975). Since then many research studies have explored different types of preparation, including a range of preparation materials and the most effective timing of and location for preparation (for example, Clough, 2005; Smith and Callery, 2005; Sutherland, 2003).

Preparation can be undertaken in many ways and by a number of the childcare professionals involved in their care, including parents. The crucial factors are that those preparing the child have the knowledge and confidence to answer their questions honestly and truthfully. Preparation for specific health issues such as cardiac-, stoma- or neuro-surgery obviously require specialist information and support, and preparation programmes specific to these areas have been developed.

Books, toys, games and dolls have been developed to assist in the preparation of children for procedures by facilitating good communication between adult and child and encouraging children to ask questions and learn about their bodies and different health care professionals. Children respond differently to preparation materials and staff may need to try a variety of approaches in order to find the best way of preparing an individual child. An important first step may be in establishing the child's own views of their information needs (Smith and Callery, 2005). Recently, computer games have been developed which facilitate preparation for children (Rassini et al., 2004) and a number of hospitals have excellent websites with information and games available for children of different ages (for example, see www.childrenfirst.nhs.uk).

Play is key to any approach to preparation and allows children an age-appropriate opportunity to be informed about and involved in decisions concerned with their health and treatment. Play in this context may be educative, normative or therapeutic (Mathison and Butterworth, 2001). Educative play gives the child information in a child-centred way about what is going to happen to them. Very few children can understand purely verbal explanations and so information must be provided and communicated in a variety of age-appropriate ways. Verbal explanations are important, however, and often accompany the use of picture books or toys, but care must be taken with the words used. Expressions such as 'you will be put to sleep for your operation' can cause fear in children who have had pets 'put to sleep' by the vet. Childcare workers often have to translate medical terms and procedures into language a child can understand but many words can have different meanings to children and their understanding should always be verified (Glasper and Haggerty, 2006).

Normative play allows the child to enjoy familiar activities in an alien situation and provides reassurance, distraction and comfort. Therapeutic play involves a two-way communication between the child and the health care professional. It enables the child to express or 'act out' their fears and anxieties both about what is going to happen and events they have experienced already. Health care professionals have an opportunity to demonstrate what is going to happen using dolls, teddies or other play equipment, and help the child to anticipate how they may feel and react. This type of behavioural rehearsal is very important in enabling children to process the information they have been given and to try out their possible responses; it provides a safe environment for communication to take place.

Communicating with parents and siblings

Having an ill child is stressful for parents. A number of research studies have explored the impact of having an ill child in an effort to identify methods of reducing parental stress levels and enabling coping. A continued source of stress for mothers was found to be the need to develop and sustain trusting relationships with staff, and good communication with staff was found to be instrumental in mothers developing coping and competence with their child's chronic illness (Swallow and Jacoby, 2001). Noyes (2000) found that the majority of mothers of critically ill children reported feelings of physical and emotional exhaustion, including nausea, headaches, shaking, episodes of crying, numbness and forgetfulness. It is clear that effective communication and engagement with parents is key to supporting them through the stressful situation of their child's illness and enabling them to cope and fulfil their roles with regard to their sick child. This is essential not only for the well-being of the parents but also because parental stress is easily communicated to children and in turn increases their levels of anxiety. Hence it is essential that professionals working in health care settings anticipate causes of parental stress and use sensitive communication to alleviate or reduce it.

Studies of parents of sick children have found that they require reassurance, information and respect for and recognition of their ability to care for their child through partnership with health professionals (Fisher, 2001; Young et al., 2002). Parents have reported both the need for more information and feeling overwhelmed by too much information (Simons and Roberson, 2002). The key to meeting parents' needs for appropriate information through effective communication is listening and being responsive to their needs. Parents become brokers of information for their child and have to facilitate their cooperation with treatment (Young et al., 2002). In their research, Simons and Roberson (2002) found that nearly half of the parents wanted more information in relation to their child's pain and its management and required help in interpreting their child's non-verbal communication regarding pain. Parents' need for information will vary over time throughout a child's illness or stay in hospital, but unfortunately key personnel such as doctors and specialist nurses are only available at specific times such as ward rounds. It is essential, therefore, that all professionals involved with the child are sensitive to the parents' needs and respond to requests for information either directly themselves or by directing them to further help. Inexperienced staff are often frightened of engaging with families of sick children as they are scared that they will be asked questions they cannot answer. Staff may create non-verbal barriers to communication and this can prevent parents from asking for help and information (ibid.). Parents can thus remain silent and this in turn is wrongly perceived by health staff as satisfaction with care. Whilst understandable, this is not defensible. Parents are well aware of the limitations of knowledge and expertise of particular staff but may lack confidence in asking for help from staff who they perceive as being busy and superior. Parents have reported dissatisfaction with medical staff who made them feel stupid and a nuisance for asking too many questions (Neill, 2000) and so it is essential that other staff listen to their needs and seek help and information on their behalf. Often parents feel more comfortable communicating with the childcare workers involved with their child on a regular basis and are more likely to share their concerns and questions with them.

Noyes (2000) found that mothers of sick children wanted to be treated with respect by all members of the multidisciplinary team. Most of the research literature has focused on the relationships between health professionals, particularly doctors, and parents when a child is sick, but relationships with all staff are significant in ensuring effective and supportive communication (Herbert and Harper Dorton, 2002).

Much publicity was given to the individual and system failures that prevented parental involvement in discussions about their children's care at Bristol Royal Infirmary and led to a drive for reform of medical practice (DoH, 2001a). There was clear criticism of the information given to parents, which was often partial, unclear and confusing. Key recommendations included ensuring that patients and parents have sufficient information to enable them to participate as partners in their care, that the information is based on current available evidence and is regularly updated, and that information is presented to patients and families in a variety of formats to enable understanding.

Siblings of sick children require special attention as they can easily feel confused and marginalised when the focus of attention is on their brother or sister who is ill. Parents may wish to protect their well children from worry and distress or may be so overwhelmed by their sick child's condition that they do not appreciate the needs of their well children. Siblings may develop their own misconceptions and fears about the sick child, particularly if the illness is sudden and/or serious. There is evidence that siblings of children with chronic illness have an increased risk of developing behavioural, emotional or mental health problems, with signs of attitude change and low self-esteem (Williams et al., 2006). However, this is not always the case; indeed, some studies have found positive consequences in siblings of sick children, who have demonstrated an increase in empathy, compassion, coping and communication skills, as well as increased maturity, appreciation of their own health and family cohesion (Elliott et al., 2006).

Childcare workers should use their communication skills to reassure, involve and inform siblings in age-appropriate ways. This may be by helping them to understand the sick child's illness and treatment but also by making siblings feel welcome and valued in health care settings. Demonstrating interest in and respect for well siblings can help them to develop trust in those caring for their family. Mathews (2006, p. 141) suggests that when communicating with families, parents should be encouraged to:

- Focus on all their children.

- Keep in contact and spend time with their other children.

- Keep siblings informed of what is happening and how their brother or sister is responding to treatment.

- Involve siblings in decision making.

- Bring siblings to the hospital and help prepare them for the visit.

Consent to health care treatment

Effective communication is central to gaining valid and informed consent from children for treatment in health care settings. Consent for medical or surgical treatment is usually obtained by a doctor and may involve obtaining written consent. However, consent must be obtained before anyone looking after a child's health can examine or treat them, although it is often done in an informal way, for example asking a child to hold out their hand so that their pulse can be taken. The Department of Health have published a number of booklets regarding obtaining consent, which provide advice and guidance for those working with children and young people (DOH, 2001b) and for children and young people themselves so that they understand their rights with regard to treatment (DoH, 2001c).

In the UK, a young person's eighteenth birthday draws a line between childhood and adulthood (Children Act 1989), after which they have the same rights as any other adult to consent to treatment. However, 16 and 17 year olds can also make decisions regarding their medical treatment independent of their parents (Family Law Reform Act 1969). Younger children also have the right to make independent decisions about their treatment, which is proportionate to their competence to make such decisions (British Medical Association, 2000). Age may be considered to be a guide as to a child's competence but it is an unreliable predictor of a child's ability to make independent decisions about medical treatment and health care.

A child's ability to consent to treatment is determined by a test of 'Gillick competence', whereby the child must demonstrate sufficient maturity and intelligence to understand and appraise the nature and implications of the proposed treatment, including the risks and alternative courses of action (Wheeler, 2006). The criteria for this 'Gillick test' were established by a judgement in the High Court in 1983 and approved by the House of Lords two years later. The test is named after a mother who challenged health service guidance that allowed her daughters, under the age of 16, to be given confidential contraceptive advice without her knowledge. However, the 'Gillick test' is applied to any situations where a child's ability to consent to treatment is assessed. It provides clinicians with an objective test of competence in order to identify children under 16 who have the legal capacity to consent to medical examination and treatment. Specific concerns in relation to providing contraceptive advice to girls under the age of 16 are addressed by the 'Fraser guidelines'. These guidelines include the necessity to ensure that the girl understands the advice given to her regarding contraception but also considers the importance of parental involvement and the risks of unprotected sex (ibid.).

A consent 'toolkit' has been developed by the British Medical Association (2008), the purpose of which is to act as a prompt to doctors when they are seeking consent by providing answers to common questions raised. It also provides guidance to all staff working with children in health care settings regarding the issues to be considered when gaining consent.

Children and young people facing life-limiting conditions

The concept of open and honest communication applies whatever the illness the child is suffering from, including life-limiting conditions. Life-limiting conditions are those illnesses which cause children to die during childhood or early adulthood. Such conditions may be evident from birth or soon after birth, such as cystic fibrosis, or develop during childhood, such as some cancers. Children with life-limiting conditions may live for many years with the condition and they and their families have to learn to manage their lives within the constraints of their illness, as well as with the knowledge that it will ultimately lead to their death.

Many childcare workers worry about what to tell children regarding their illness and conversations about death in particular cause a great deal of anxiety. It is important that staff are aware that evidence suggests that honesty and openness are beneficial not only to the children but their families when facing life-limiting conditions (Lansdown, 1998). In the past, parents and health care staff have tried to protect children from the seriousness of their condition, believing that the less children were aware, the less frightened and distressed they would be. However, researchers as far back as the 1970s identified that even those children who were protected from the 'truth' and were not told specifically about their condition gathered a considerable amount of information about their disease, including the possibility of death (Blubond-Lagner, 1978). Information gathered in such a way, however, is often distorted and incomplete and may increase the child's feelings of confusion, fear and loneliness. Children may even find themselves in the situation of pretending to know less than they do in order to protect their parents and adult carers from difficult and distressing conversations.

In spite of awareness of the importance of honesty and openness staff can still find it difficult to talk to children about their condition. Childcare professionals may be afraid of the child's reaction and being blamed for the situation. They may find it difficult to explain and handle the uncertainty of the situation and be scared of expressing their own emotions (Lansdown, 1998). It is easy to forget the two-way nature of communication when the issues are so difficult, but staff must remember to be tuned in to the child's response as much as to their own need to give information. Non-verbal responses are often more informative than words and children will show their response in a variety of ways. It is important that feelings as well as facts are conveyed and childcare workers can communicate a great deal by their own gestures and expressions.

Lansdown (ibid., p. 94) suggests four key aspects to effective communication about death:

1. The need for awareness of the developmental level of the child.

2. The value of appreciating the existing communication system within the family.

3. The realisation that effective communication can reduce anxiety.

4. The choice of medium of communication most easily used by the child.

C H A P T E R   S U M M A R Y

Every episode of communication in health care settings is significant to the children and families in our care (Carter, 2009). Communicating with children, young people and their families in health care settings and contexts poses particular challenges and rewards for childcare workers. The need for effective communication is explored in this chapter with particular regard to children's understanding of health and access to and involvement in health care. The need for sound communication skills when caring for children who are sick and in pain has been explored and particular issues regarding gaining consent for treatment and procedures considered.

Parents' involvement in the care of children in health care settings is a crucial factor in delivering safe and effective care. They have particular needs with regard to communication, and childcare workers must ensure that they communicate information in appropriate ways and at appropriate times in order to reduce their anxiety and stress and promote successful coping with their child's illness.

FURTHER READING

Chambers, R and Licence, K (eds) (2005) *Looking after children in primary care*. Oxford: Radcliffe Publishing.

This book is a companion to the Children's National Service Framework enabling those working in primary care at the interface between the NHS, education and social services to put the NSF into practice.

Department of Health, Department for Children, Schools and Families (2009) *Healthy lives, brighter future: The strategy for children and young people's health*. London: Department of Health.

Published in February 2009 this joint DH/DCSF strategy presents the government's vision for children and young people's health and wellbeing.

Glasper, A and Richardson, J (eds) (2006) *A textbook of children's and young people's nursing*. London: Elsevier.

Although aimed at children's nurses this is a key British text book on child-centred healthcare within a family context.

Chapter 7

Communication with children: The legal dimensions

Eileen Wake

Objectives

By the end of this chapter, you should have an understanding of:

- The legal and ethical aspects of communication.
- Children's rights and vulnerabilities within the context of their everyday lives.
- The impact of key legislation and child welfare.

Introduction

This chapter explores some elements of the complex legal and ethical aspects of communication with children and young people. For practitioners, it is important that children and young people have the same rights as adults in terms of communicating with them. Indeed, they have additional child-orientated rights due to their inherent vulnerability as children as they depend on adults for care, protection, support and love. Children have the right to explanations regarding decision making relating to their health, care and education, and for these to be made in a developmentally appropriate manner. This chapter will explore the impact of key legislation on child welfare from a national and international perspective to enable the reader to evaluate how they communicate with children and young people in their everyday lives. As UNICEF (2009, p. 1) highlights: 'children are not the property of their parents nor are they helpless objects of charity. They are human beings and are the subject of their own rights.' This is the cornerstone to this chapter and reflects the rights of children holistically and within the context of their everyday lives as members of families, as schoolchildren and as members of their communities.

The United Nations Convention on the Rights of the Child (1989) encompasses a wide range of universal rights for children and young people, which practitioners must have a sound knowledge of. These are outlined on Unicef's excellent website (www.unicef.org). However, a 2008 Unicef review of how countries have faired in terms of meeting the rights of children highlighted that 3 million children in the UK live in poverty and we have higher infant mortality rates than other similar countries; this raises issues for us all in terms of ensuring that children's needs are better communicated in actual assessed outcomes that directly enhance their lives. This is reinforced clearly in the UK Children's Commissioners report to the UN (Aynsley-Green, 2008a) and the annual review of children's rights in the UK by the Children's Rights Alliance for England (CRAE, 2008). Readers are encouraged to review the work of the Children's Commissioners in the UK in order to aid their understanding of the current work being undertaken to raise the public profile of childhood, children and young people.

The best interests of the child should be the cornerstone of all health, education and social care. The best interests principle in caring and supporting children and young people and ensuring that their universal and individual rights are being met is enshrined within the United Nations Convention on the Rights of the Child (1989; UNICEF, 2009) and nationally within the Children Act 1989, 2004, the Children (Scotland) Act 1995 and the Human Rights Act 1998. Indeed, the Human Rights Act 1998 clearly identifies that children have the right to protection, participation and family life; to have decisions that affect them always to be in their best interests; and, of course, to be involved in making these decisions to the best of their abilities. However at times it can feel that the best interests of children are subsumed into the generic policies and needs of the adult population. There are 11 million children and young people in the UK (Aynsley-Green, 2008a) and yet they continue to experiences services that are adult rather than child and young people orientated. The Children's Plan (DCSF, 2007a, 2008b, 2008c) and Children Act 2004 clearly highlight that all staff working with children and young people must have appropriate training in communication, as well as specifically in relation to child protection.

So . . . who is a child?

One would think that this would be straightforward and does not need to be considered; however, in reality in the UK, it is a source of much confusion and results in children being viewed differently by the statutory agencies. For example, the age of criminal responsibility in England, Wales and Northern Ireland is ten (Crime and Disorder Act 1998, Section 34) and is as low as eight in Scotland (Criminal Procedure (Scotland) Act 1995, Section 41), both when a child is still at primary school; although much discussion has taken place (Scottish Law Commission, 2001) and it is anticipated that this will now be raised to 12 years in Scotland (MacAskill, 2009). This is in direct comparison with the age that a child is deemed capable of being able to make decisions regarding their own health care, as children and young people under the age of 16 have to demonstrate that they have the capacity to fully understand the decision they are about to make (*Gillick v West Norfolk and Wisbech AHA* [1986] AC 112 (DoH, 2001b; General Medical Council, 2007). This is explored further in Chapter 6 in relation to health care. Also, a young person cannot make the decision to leave school until 18, marry before the age of 16, vote or have a tattoo until 18 (Education and Skills Act 2008; Age of Marriage Act 1929; Electoral Commission 2006; Tattooing of Minors Act 1969), yet can be held criminally responsible. Understandably, there has been much ongoing debate (Allen, 2006; Broadbridge, 2009) regarding the age of responsibility, and the United Nations Committee on the Rights of the Child (2008) questioned the decision making regarding this. In addition, in terms of accessing education, until recently a child could leave at the age of 16 (Education Act 1996); however, under the new Education and Skills Act 2008, the leaving age will be raised to 18 by 2015, and all children entering secondary school from September 2008 will be affected.

In terms of communication with children and young people, practitioners must ensure that they do not give them mixed messages regarding their value as children first and foremost whilst simultaneously expecting them to take on board and use adult decision-making skills in their daily lives. This is highlighted in the way in which consent to health and social care, particularly health care, has been developed. The importance of giving informed consent to treatment that is not coerced by others has been explored in Chapter 6. The notion of being competent to make your own health care decisions (the 'Gillick test') when under the age of 16 has resulted in key guidance being issued to help practitioners in communicating with young people regarding their capacity to give consent (DoH, Social Services Public Safety, 2003; GMC 2007).

Significant changes have occurred in the way that the law now addresses the needs of those over the age of 16 in terms of informed consent and communication in relation to health and/or social care. Whilst the Family Law Reform Act 1969 is still on the statute books, the Mental Capacity Act 2005 came into force in 2007 and requires practitioners to consider a young person over the age of 16 to be competent to provide consent for themselves (what is termed, a presumption of capacity) unless it can be clearly identified that they are not able to do so (for example, a young person with a severe learning disability; Mencap, 2004). However, what is important here in terms of communication, is that practitioners must demonstrate that they know how to support young people in their decision making through effective and therapeutic communication skills and can demonstrate that they have consulted with the young person, and utilised communication strategies appropriate to their developmental needs. This can and should include the use of augmentative and alternative communication strategies to ensure that the young person's wishes and choices are known. For young people with severe mental health problems, there may be concerns regarding their capacity to make decisions about their own treatment at times when the illness is at its most severe (more usually known as fluctuating capacity; Mental Capacity Act 2005). Therefore, where possible, if decisions can be delayed until the young person is well, this is advised. If, however, there are concerns about the young person's health and well-being that could be exacerbated or are unlikely to be resolved unless treatment is initiated, then care and treatment will need to be provided without their consent (what is termed, treatment as an act of necessity, where there is reasonable belief that the young person is unable to make this decision for themselves; General Medical Council 2007; Mental Capacity Act 2005).

Formal advocacy support is provided through the courts where a young person lacks capacity in the form of a Public Guardian and what is termed the Independent Mental Capacity Advocate, who will be responsible for ensuring that the best interests of the young person are clearly communicated to all who need to know and will challenge any decision making that is not felt to have been made in their best interests. Any decisions that require legal consideration regarding the capacity of an individual will be via the Court of Protection. This raises an important issue in terms of communication with and for children and young people – that of advocacy and the need for practitioners to understand that their duty of care is to the child/young person and that their welfare is paramount (Children Act 1989, 2004).

Advocacy is a key element of ensuring that the rights of children and young people are met (UN Convention on the Rights of the Child, Article 12) and is defined by the Independent Advocacy Commission as 'taking action to help people say what they want, secure their rights, represent their interests and obtain services they need' (Lewington and Clipson, 2001, p. 4). It is an important area of everyday communication in working with children and young people for all practitioners, yet is often inadequately acknowledged (Chase et al., 2006; DoH, 2002a, b, 2004a, b; Lewington and Clipson, 2001; Oliver et al., 2006).

The Department of Health (2002a) published national standards for children's advocacy services in order to gain consistency in provision across the UK and to ensure that the service is available to all children and young people being cared for in the looked-after system and/or who are in need (Children Act 1989). These services are available for young people up to 21 years of age (Wyld, 2002). The standards cite advocacy for children and young people as 'speaking up' for them, empowering them 'to make sure that their rights are respected and their views and wishes are heard at all times' (DoH, 2002a, p. 9). The Department of Health (2001b) highlighted that children and young people in the looked-after system are 'amongst the most socially excluded groups in England' (p. 3), in that they have greater health needs than children and young people of similar age but are less likely to receive adequate health care, particularly regarding their mental health. This raises a number of communication issues, both for practitioners working with the children and young people and also for practitioners working with other agencies to ensure that their needs are being met. In addition, children and young people being cared for within the looked-after system are also considered vulnerable in terms of risk of harm, potentially from workers and/or peers, as acknowledged in a number of high profile studies and reports (Barter et al., 2004; Bunting, 2005; Waterhouse, 2000). Therefore, the notion of advocacy for these children and young people is not optional and has to be inherent in all aspects of their care. The implication for practitioners is that they remain focused on their duty of care within services for children and young people – that is, supporting them, using active listening and advocacy skills and ensuring that their welfare is always the most important aspect of their work.

However, as acknowledged by Oliver et al. (2006), whilst it is absolutely imperative that advocacy services be integral to services for children and young people in the looked-after system, advocacy should be available for all children and young people. This should be possible but requires practitioners to revisit their attitudes, beliefs and values when working with children and young people in order to ensure it becomes implicit in all aspects of health and social care and education. Indeed, advocacy is evident in schools with pupil-led school councils, in both primary and secondary education, where children and young people are encouraged to express their feelings and wishes in terms of school activities and these are then taken on board. Practitioners must ensure that children and young people's views, wishes and needs are heard, and that they have all the information they need to make necessary choices.

How a child/young person is defined also impacts on the type of health and social care provision that is accessed, and means that young people aged 16 and 17 years are often in what can only be described as a 'no man's land' in terms of accessing services such as health; they are no longer able to access paediatric services as a first referral but adult services are not appropriate and do not always have the necessary expertise to meet their needs. This is emphasised in 'Pushed into the shadows', a report by the Children's Commissioner for England, Aynsley-Green (2007), which highlighted that young people with mental health needs were being inappropriately cared for in adult mental health wards. Young people in the study felt left out of decisions that affected their care and, worryingly, some felt unsafe in these units and had suffered verbal, physical and/or sexual abuse by adult patients. A number of recommendations were made, including a commitment that no young person will be cared for in an adult mental health ward/unit by 2010. Some of the recommendations have now been enacted to some extent; however, the latest report (Aynsley-Green, 2008b) highlighted that some young people are still experiencing these problems.

From a communication perspective, therefore, there is a clear need for advocacy in services to meet the needs of young people; for practitioners to listen to young people and to act upon the concerns raised. This can be achieved in a multitude of ways, including through art, drama and leisure activities, and more formal strategies such as focus groups and specific empowerment projects (McGee and Barn, 2007). One organisation that has sought to address this is the National Youth Advocacy Service (www.nyas.net/aboutus.html), which provides advice, advocacy and legal services specifically for young people to ensure that their wishes are heard and given due attention; for example, in court where a young person's best interests may be debated (*Mabon v Mabon and Others* [2005] EWCA Civ 634). The Children's Rights Alliance for England (CRAE, www.crae.org.uk) is another excellent organisation and provides a range of resources to assist practitioners in working in partnership with children and young people. It is part of a group of organisations seeking to enhance communication with children and young people and to increase their participation in decisions made about them by agencies (Participation Works, 2009). One important campaign launched in March 2009 by CRAE is that of working with journalists to promote children's rights in the UK within the media and thus within the public as a whole.

Communicating concerns or advocacy issues

Whilst the child/young person has the same rights as an adult in terms of confidentiality (DoH, 2003c; GMC, 2007; Royal College of General Practitioners, 2000), there are times when information needs to be shared with professionals and other agencies in order to meet their best interests. This may be because the child is in need (Children Act 1989, Section 17) and input from a range of agencies is required, or where the child/young person is at risk or has suffered significant emotional, physical and/or sexual harm (DCSF, 2008g). Practitioners who have any concerns about whether a child/young person is at risk or has suffered harm must follow their agency's safeguarding procedures. Students on placement must inform their mentor or a senior practitioner as a matter of urgency – if in doubt, they must communicate their concerns and justification for them. It can be difficult if the child/young person has told a practitioner or student about what has happened to them or that they are worried may happen to them and asks them not to tell anyone else. However whilst confidentiality is always an important element of communication with children and young people, the practitioner does have a duty to share these concerns in order to protect their well-being. This needs to be explained in a sensitive and thoughtful way, using developmentally appropriate language.

Staying safe is a key element of *Every Child Matters* (DCSF, 2008f) and the Children Act 2004, and all children have the right to be safe from maltreatment, neglect, violence and sexual exploitation. After the deaths of Holly Wells and Jessica Chapman in 2002, the Bichard Inquiry Report (2004) identified a wide range of actions that needed to be undertaken by agencies, including ways of improving communication across agencies. This was also in tangent with the Sexual Offences Act 2003, which came into force in 2004. From a communication perspective, practitioners need to understand that:

1. Consent to sexual activity is now legally defined and adults cannot make assumptions of consent. Adults now have to provide sound evidence that the person they have been involved in sexual activities with was over the age of 18 years.

2. Children under the age of 13 years can now never legally consent to sexual activity

---

CASE STUDY

You are working as a teaching assistant in a secondary school. Fiona, aged 14, quietly asks to talk to you. Her friends have said that you would listen and help her. Fiona starts to cry and talks about her mum's boyfriend who has been taking photos of her getting dressed and undressed. She doesn't know what to do about it.

Comment

The above scenario is designed to encourage the reader to think about their communication skills, how to support a child/young person who is distressed, the confidentiality issues and their duty of care to protect this young person. It also allows the reader to reflect on their knowledge base regarding child protection and the policies/protocols in the school setting in relation to communicating concerns regarding harm. It would be useful for the reader to map out what they would do next and why, and to share this exercise with a colleague to enable them to explore the issues in greater depth.

Whilst ensuring practitioners working with children and young people are mindful of the Sexual Offences Act 2003, it is important that the sexual health needs of young people are also considered. Those supporting young people who are involved in sexual activity should offer appropriate sexual and reproductive health advice and information regarding where to go for contraception or treatment (DCSF, 2007b). This should be undertaken together with GPs and school nurses, and due regard given to the child protection issues that may arise. Practitioners working with young people in the statutory and non-statutory sectors must consider communication in these circumstances in terms of how they would respond when asked for, for example, information regarding contraception advice. Where could they get advice for both themself and the young person? What potential issues may arise in terms of seeking to support the young person?

You are working within young people's leisure services and have built up good relationships with the young people, as you have been helping them with a street dance production. One evening, Jack, who is 12, asks you if you know anything about 'being safe' as he and his girlfriend want to have sex; he also asks you not to tell anyone. He says he hasn't tried it yet but he and his girlfriend have been talking about sex a lot.

- *How are you going to reply to Jack?*
- *What will you do next and why?*
- *How can you work with Jack to explore the issues and choices he faces?*
- *What impact do you think peer pressure has on young people wanting to have sex?*
- *How are you going to share your concerns with Jack?*

Comment

The above scenario is designed to prompt the reader to reflect upon how they would communicate with Jack and where they would go for advice and support for both Jack and themselves. The reader should be reassured that there are always professionals available for advice and support and they would not need to deal with such a situation alone. Dealing with the situation alone would also be unfair to Jack and his girlfriend and would breach current legislation and policies for safeguarding children. Practitioners/students should always share their concerns and seek advice.

Intra- and inter-agency communication to meet the needs of children and young people

Communication across and within agencies working with children, young people and their families should be effective and consistent. Unfortunately, there are a number of examples of a child's best interests not being met because of basic communication failures within agencies – even when the child is known to the agencies concerned. A recent, though rare, example is the ongoing case concerning the alleged sexual assault by a fostered 18 year old of the foster family's two-year-old child; the 18 year old had a history of sexual assault (Lombard, 2009).

The use of the Common Assessment Framework (Children's Workforce Development Council (CDWC), 2007) and the resultant multidisciplinary and agency assessment in partnership with the family is supposed to ensure that the child/young person remains the main focus of care and support. However, this has yet to be come universally used by all agencies and some are still using alternative documentation that can mean information is not shared effectively. Contact Point (DCSF, 2009) is the new national information sharing index and was meant to be effective from 2009 (it has been delayed due to technology issues). It was developed as a consequence of the Laming Report (2003), Every Child Matters (DCSF, 2008c, 2008d) and the Children Act 2004.

Communication issues – information sharing

Every Child Matters (DSCF, 2008d, 2008e, 2008f) highlighted the key areas that must be considered when sharing information about a child/young person and their family. These include the need to be open and honest with them regarding what, how and why information will be shared. The child's safety and welfare is of paramount concern whenever a decision is made to share information with other agencies – it has to be the key to all communication issues for practitioners. Respecting the child/young person's wishes is crucial and wherever possible and appropriate their consent must be sought. Consent must not be sought at the expense of the child's best interests, however, and in some cases can be over-ridden; this outcome and an explanation must be clearly documented in the child's records.

Information sharing is complex and is governed by a multitude of legislation and policies. In terms of legislation alone this includes a rather long list and these are only some of the key Acts, for example, as highlighted in the excellent DCSF guidance in relations to information sharing (2009, pp. 11–21): 'Children Act 1989, 2004, Local Government Act 2000, Education Act 1996, 2002, Learning and Skills Act 2000, Education (Special Educational Needs) Regulations 2001, Children (Leaving Care Act) 2000, Protection of Children Act 1999, Immigration and Asylum Act 1999, Crime and Disorder Act 1998, National Health Service Act 1977, Health and Social Care Act 2003, Human Rights Act 1998, Data Protection Act 1998 – as well as the common law duty of confidentiality (Information Commission Office, 2006)'.

Therefore, working with children, young people and their families requires your written communication to be accurate, contemporaneous, stored safely using the guidelines for the organisation you are working within and only shared with appropriate named others. If you are at all unsure about whether you should share information regarding a child or young person you must seek advice within the organisation that you are working for and the decision must be recorded in the child's records (Bichard, 2003; DCSF, 2008d, 2008e, 2008f; Kennedy, 2001).

ACTIVITY 7.1

One area of advocacy that raises ethical concern is that of meeting the advocacy needs of parents/carers who are being investigated under the Children Act 1989 (Section 47).

- *What issues do you think a practitioner working with the family may have to deal with?*

- *Review the current protocol for parents (child protection) by Lindley and Richards (2002) on behalf of the DoH (available at www.dh.gov.uk/en/publicationsandstatements/ Publications/PublicationsPolicyandGuidance/DH_4127568). How can the guidance help you understand the issues that you have raised?*

Comment

This activity is designed to encourage the reader to explore their understanding of advocacy and the difficulties practitioners may encounter in communicating with families regarding their concerns about the child's welfare. Practitioners must remain focused on their duty of care to the child whilst working with the family.

The reader needs to review the above activity in conjunction with the reports and guidance relating to the death of 'Baby P' in 2007 (DCSF 2008g; Haringey Local Safeguarding Children Board, 2008). They should also review the subsequent guidance provided by Lord Laming (2009) regarding safeguarding children, which highlights again the importance of effective communication amongst practitioners, not just with families but with colleagues and line managers as well as other agencies. These communication issues sadly are not new, and have been the recommendation of many reports in relation to child protection and the non-accidental death of children, for example Victoria Climbié (DoH, 2003b; Laming, 2003). A number of changes were instigated to protect children following this case, particularly in relation to inter-agency working, which led to the development of the Children Act 2004. Staying safe – one of the key principles of Every Child Matters (DCSF, 2008g) – is still not a reality for all children, as highlighted by the NSPCC (2008). Practitioners thus need to focus more on keeping children safe and protecting them from harm, which means being responsible and accountable for their communication regarding the welfare of children. Lord Laming's (2009) progress report regarding child protection again highlights the importance of communication in relation to child protection. There are 58 recommendations within the report and the reader should review them as an adjunct to this chapter. Communication is a recurrent theme – with children and their families, with colleagues and between agencies, as well as written communication. Current integrated systems must work to better protect children and young people. The report states that assessment needs to take into account all significant events in the child's life and evidence from all practitioners who have or are involved in supporting the child, and involve direct contact with the child. Again, it is all about communication and the importance of not assuming that the child's best interests are always being met by the support put in place by agencies.

CHAPTER SUMMARY

This chapter continues the theme that every child really does matter and highlights not only the legal elements of communication and what legislation influences practice, but also the ultimate potential consequences of poor communication by practitioners for the child/young person. The best interests and the rights of the child/young person should always be paramount and central to everyday practice by all who work with children and young people. Communication is not a luxury; it is a necessity.

This chapter includes a wide range of areas in which the reader is encouraged to explore further. A number of the websites have been highlighted in the chapter that include a wealth of information, advice and interactive materials to enhance understanding. Again the reader is advised to maximise their understanding of the *Every Child Matters* agenda issues by accessing the website on a regular basis. Further reading in terms of textbooks has been chosen in terms of those which build upon the skills and knowledge of the reader, which includes:

FURTHER READING

Alderson, P (2008) *Young children's rights: Exploring beliefs, principles and practice.* 2nd edition. London: Jessica Kingsley.

Easy to review and will make you think about your practice in relation to the rights of younger children.

Children's Rights Alliance for England (CRAE) (2008) *State of children's rights in England 2008*. London: CRAE.

Places current issues regarding children and childhood in the UK in an international context.

Children's Workforce Development Council (CWDC) (2007) *Common assessment framework for children and young people: Practitioner's guide. Integrated working to improve outcomes for children and young people*. London: CWDC.

Important to review in terms of inter-professional working.

Davis, L (2008) *The social worker's guide to children and families law*. London: Jessica Kingsley. A useful guide.

General Medical Council (2007) *0–18 years: Guidance for all doctors*. London: GMC.

Useful to review in terms of consent to health care – also available on the GMC website to download for personal use www.gmc.org.uk.

Read, JM, Clements, L and Ruebain, D (2006) *Disabled children and the law: Research and good practice*. 2nd edition. London: Jessica Kingsley.

Easy to read and thought provoking.

Essential reading in terms of the protection of children and your responsibilities:

Department of Health (2003) *Checklist of practice recommendations from the Victoria Climbié inquiry*. London: DoH.

Kennedy, I (2001) *The inquiry into the management of care of children receiving complex heart surgery at the Bristol Royal Infirmary*. www.bristol-inquiry.org.uk.

Laming, Lord (2003) *The Victoria Climbié inquiry*. www.victoria-climbié-inquiry.org.uk.

Laming, Lord (2009) *The protection of children in England: A progress report*. London: Stationery Office.

WEBSITES

www.11million.org.uk
www.actionforchildren.org.uk
www.barnardos.org.uk
www.bichard.inquiry.org
www.bristol-inquiry.org.uk
www.childrenslawcentre.org
www.edcm.org.uk
www.everychildmatters.gov.uk
www.mencap.org.uk
www.ncb.org.uk
www.nspcc.org.uk/inform
www.opsi.gov.uk/Acts
www.savethechildren.org.uk
www.rights4me.org

Bibliography

Age of Marriage Act (1929) hansard.millbanksystems.com

Ainscow, M, Booth, T and Dyson, A (1999) Inclusion and exclusion in schools: Listening to some hidden voices. In Ballard, K (ed.) *Inclusive education: International voices on disability and justice*. London: Falmer Press.

Ainscow, M, Booth, T and Dyson, A (2006) *Improving schools, developing inclusion*. London: Routledge.

Ainscow, M and Kaplan, I (2005) Using evidence to encourage inclusive school development: possibilities and challenges. *Australasian Journal of Special Education, 29* (2):12–21.

Ainsworth, MDS, Blehar, MC, Waters, E and Wall, S (1978) *Patterns of attachment: A psychological study of the strange situation*. Hillsdale, NJ: Erlbaum.

Alcock, P, Erskine, A and May, M (2003) *The student's companion to social policy*. London: Social Policy Association.

Allan, J (1999) *Actively seeking inclusion*. London: Falmer Press.

Allen, R (2006) *From punishment to problem-solving: A new approach to children in trouble*. www.crimereduction.home office.gov.uk

Ammentorp, J, Mainz, J and Sabroe, S (2005) Parents' priorities and satisfaction with acute pediatric care. *Archives of Pediatrics and Adolescent Medicine*, 159: 127–31.

Anning, A, Cottrell, D, Frost, N, Green, J and Robinson, M (2006) *Developing multiprofessional teamwork for integrated children's services*. Maidenhead: Open University Press.

Armstrong, D, Armstrong, F and Barton, L (2000) Introduction: what is this book about. In Armstrong, F, Armstrong, D and Barton, L (eds) *Inclusive education: policy, contexts and comparative perspectives*. London: David Fulton.

Arnold, E (2007) Intercultural communication. In Arnold, EC and Underman-Boggs, K (eds) *Interprofessional relationships: Professional communication skills for nurses*, 5th edition. St Louis: Saunders Elsevier.

Aynsley-Green, A (2007) *'Pushed into the shadows' – young people's experience of adult mental health facilities*. www.11million.org.uk

Aynsley-Green, A (2008a) *11 million children and young people in England have the right to a voice*. www.11million.org.uk

Aynsley-Green, A (2008b) *Out of the shadows? A review of the responses to recommendations made in 'Pushed into the Shadows': Young people's experience of adult mental health facilities*. www.11million.org.uk

Azarnoff, P (1976) The care of children in hospitals: An overview. *Journal of Pediatric Psychology*, 1: 5–6.

Baggens, C (2001) What they talk about: Conversations between child health centre nurses and parents. *Journal of Advanced Nursing*, 36(5): 659–67.

Ballard, K (1997) Researching disability and inclusive education: Participation, construction and interpretation. *International Journal of Inclusive Education*, 1(3): 243–56.

Balls, E (2008) Statement on safeguarding of children. 1 December. London: Department of Children, Schools and Families.

Bandura, A (1977) *Social learning theory*. London: Prentice Hall.

Barker, R. (2009) *Making sense of Every Child Matters*. Bristol: Policy Press.

Barlow, J and Underdown, A (2005) Promoting the social and emotional health of children: Where now? *Journal of the Royal Society for the Promotion of Health*, 125(2): 64–70.

Baron-Cohen, S, Golan, O, Chapman, E and Granader, Y (2007) Transported into a world of emotion. *The Psychologist*, 20(2): 76–7.

Barter, C, Renold, E, Berridge, D and Cawson, P (2004) *Peer violence in children's residential care*. Basingstoke: Palgrave Macmillan.

Barton, L (1997) Inclusive education: Romantic, subversive or realistic?. *International Journal of Inclusive Education*, 1(3): 231–242.

BEAT (Beating Eating Disorders) (2009a) *Together we will beat eating disorders*. London: BEAT.

BEAT (2009b) *Choice or chance? Ending the information lottery*. Norwich: BEAT.

Bichard, M (2004) *The Bichard inquiry report*. London: Stationery Office; www.bichard.inquiry.org

Blakemore, K (2003). *Social policy: An introduction*. 2nd edition. Buckingham: Open University Press.

Blubond-Lagner, M (1978) *The private worlds of dying children*. Princeton, NJ: Princeton University Press.

Bochel, HM, Bochel, C, Page, R and Sykes, R (2005) *Social policy: Issues and developments*. Harlow: Prentice Hall.

Bone, M and Meltzer, H (1989) *The prevalence of disability among children: OPCS surveys of disability in Great Britain. Technical Report 3*. London: Office of Population Censuses and Surveys.

Booth, T and Ainscow, M (1998) *From them to us*. London: Routledge.

Bowlby, JER (1951 *Maternal care and mental health*. Geneva: World Health Organisation.

Bowlby, JER (1965) *Child care and the growth of love*. Harmondsworth: Penguin.

Bowlby, JER (1969) *Attachment and loss*. London: Hogarth Press.

Bowlby, JER (1979) *The making and breaking of affectional bonds*. London: Tavistock.

Bowlby, JER (1988) *A secure base: Clinical applications of attachment theory*. London: Routledge.

British Medical Association (2000) *Consent, rights and choices in health care for children and young people*. London: BMJ Publishing.

British Medical Association (2008) *Consent toolkit*. www.bma.org.uk

Broadbridge, S (2009) *The age of criminal responsibility in England and Wales*. SN/HA/3001 House of Commons Home Affairs Section. London: Stationery Office.

Brom, D, Pat-Horenczyk, R and Ford, JD (eds) (2008) *Treating traumatised children: Risk, resilience and recovery*. London: Routledge.

Bronfenbrenner U (ed.) (2005) *Making human beings human: Bioecological perspectives on human development*. London: Sage.

Brookes, H for the NSPCC (2009) *Children talking to ChildLine about suicide*. London: NSPCC. www.nspcc.org.uk

Bruner, J (1980) *Under five in Britain: A report from the Oxford pre-school research project*. Ypsilanti, MI: High/Scope Press.

Bunting, L (2005*) Females who sexually offend against children: Responses of the child protection and criminal justice system*. London: NSPCC.

Burden, T, Cooper, C and Petrie, S (2000) *'Modernising' social policy: Unravelling New Labour's welfare reforms*. Aldershot: Ashgate.

Butler, I (2002) A code of ethics for social work and social care research. *British Journal of Social Work*, 32(5): 239–48.

Byrne, D (2006) *Social exclusion.* 2nd edition. Maidenhead: Open University Press.

Calabrese, A and Burgelman Lanham, J-C (eds) (1999) *Communication, citizenship, and social policy: Rethinking the limits of the welfare state.* London: Rowman & Littlefield.

Carr, A (ed.) (2000) *'What works with children and adolescents?' A critical review of psychological interventions with children, adolescents and their families.* London: Brunner-Routledge.

Carr, A (2006) *The handbook of child and adolescent clinical psychology: A contextual approach.* 2nd edition. London: Routledge.

Cassidy, J and Shaver, PR (2008) *Handbook of attachment: Theory, research and clinical applications.* London: Guilford Press.

Chambers, R (2007) Involving children and young people in how healthcare is organized. In Chambers, R and Licence, K (eds) *Looking after children in primary care.* Oxford: Radcliffe Publishing.

Charlton, T (1996) Listening to pupils in classrooms and schools. In Davie, R and Galloway, D (eds) *Listening to children in education.* London: David Fulton.

Chase, E, Simon, A, Wigfall, V, Warwick, I and Heathcote, S (2006) *Voice advocacy service evaluation findings.* London: University of London.

Children Act 1989. www.opsi.gov.uk

Children Act 2004. www.opsi.gov.uk

Children (Leaving Care) Act 2000. www.opsi.gov.uk

Children's Rights Alliance for England (CRAE) (2008) *State of children's rights in England report 2008.* London: CRAE.

CRAE (2009) *Another perspective: A guide to assist journalists in promoting children's human rights and equality.* 2 March. London: CRAE.; www.actionforadvocacy.org.uk

Children's Workforce Development Council (CWDC) (2008) *Integrated working explained.* Leeds: CWDC.

CWDC (2007) *Common assessment framework for children and young people: Practitioner's guide. Integrated working to improve outcomes for children and young people.* London: CWDC.

Churchill, D and McPherson, A (2005) Getting it right in primary care: creating a child and young person friendly environment. In Chambers, R and Licence, K (eds) *Looking after children in primary care.* Oxford: Radcliffe Publishing.

Churchill, RD, Allen J, Pringle, M et al. (2000) Do the attitudes and beliefs of young teenagers towards General Practice influence actual consultation behaviour? *British Journal of General Practice,* 50: 953–57.

Clarke-Stewart, A (1998) The NICHD study of early child care. *Psychiatric Times,* 15(3).

Clements, A, Fletcher, D and Parry-Landon, N (2007) *Three years on: Survey of the emotional development and well-being of children and young people.* London: Office of National Statistics; www.statistics.gov.uk

Clipson, C and Lewington, W (2003) *Advocating for equality.* London: Scope, on behalf of the Independent Advocacy Campaign.

Clough, J (2005) Using books to prepare children for surgery. *Paediatric Nursing,* 17(9): 28–30.

Clunies-Ross, L (1997) Where have all the children gone? An analysis of new statistical data on sight problems amongst children in England, Scotland and Wales. *British Journal of Sight Problems,* 15: 48–53.

Coad, J and Houston, R (2007) *Involving children and young people in decision-making processes of healthcare services.* London: Action for Sick Children.

Coad, JE and Shaw, KL (2008) Is children's choice in health care rhetoric or reality? A scoping review. *Journal of Advanced Nursing*, 64(4): 318–27.

Coles, B. (2000) *Joined-up youth research, policy and practice: A new agenda for change?* Leicester: Youth Work Press.

Coles, B, Britton, L and Hicks, L (2004), *Building better connections: Inter-agency work and the connexions strategy.* Bristol: Policy Press.

Cooper, C (2008) *Community, conflict and the State: Rethinking notions of, 'safety', 'cohesion' and 'wellbeing'.* Basingstoke: Palgrave MacMillan.

Craig, G (1989) Community and the State, *Community Development Journal*, 24:1, 3–18.

Crime and Disorder Act 1998. www.opsi.gov.uk

Crow, G, Foley, P and Leverett, S (2008) Communicating with children. In Foley, P and Leverett, S (eds) *Connecting with children*. Bristol: Policy Press.

Dahlberg G, Moss, P and Pence AR (1999) *Beyond quality in early childhood education and care*. London and Philadelphia, PA: Falmer Press.

Data Protection Act 1998. www.opsi.gov.uk

Davie, R and Galloway, D (1996) The voice of the child in education. In Davie, R and Galloway, D (eds) *Listening to children in education*. London: David Fulton.

Davies, B (1999) *From Thatcherism to New Labour: A history of the Youth Service in England, Volume 2 1979–1999.* Leicester: Youth Work Press.

Davies, L (2000) Researching democratic understanding in primary school. *Research in Education*, 61: 39–48.

Davis, P (2000) Understanding children's views about reading. Unpublished PhD thesis, University of Manchester.

Department for Children, Schools and Families (DCSF) (2007a) *The children's plan. Building brighter futures.* London: Stationery Office.

DCSF (2007b) *Improving access to sexual health services for young people in further education settings.* London: DCSF, DoH.

DCSF (2008) *Every child matters outcome framework*. London: DSCF; publications.everychildmatters.gov.uk

DCSF (2008a) Early years foundation stage. London: Stationery Office

DCSF (2008b) *The children's plan: One year on – progress report*. London: DCSF.

DCSF (2008c) *Children's plan framework: A practitioner's guide*. London: DCSF.

DCSF (2008d) *Building brighter futures: Next steps for the children's workforce*. London: DCSF.

DCSF (2008e) *Information sharing: Guidance for practitioners and managers*. London. DCSF; www.publications.every childmatters.gov.uk

DCSF (2008f) *Making it happen: Working together for children, young people and families*. London: DCSF; www. publications.everychildmatters.gov.uk

DCSF (2008g) *Staying safe: Action plan*. London: DCSF.

DCSF (2008h) Ed Balls statement on safeguarding children. Available at www.dcsf.gov

DCSF (2009) *Information sharing: Further guidance on legal issues*. www.everychildmatters.gov.uk

Department for Education and Skills (DfES) (2001) *Special educational needs code of practice.* London: Stationery Office.

DfES (2003) *Every child matters*, Green Paper. London: Stationery Office.

DfES (2003) *Every child matters*. London: Stationery Office.

DfES (2004a) *The common assessment framework*. London: Stationary Office.

DfES (2004b) *Pupil characteristics and class sizes in maintained schools in England*. London: Department for Education and Skills.

DfES (2005a) *Youth matters*. London: Stationery Office.

DfES (2005b) *Common core of skills and knowledge for the children's workforce*. London: Stationery Office. www.everychildmatters.gov.uk

DfES (2007) *Care matters. Time for change: A summary*. London: Stationery Office.

DfES and Department of Health (2004) *National service framework for children, young people and maternity services: Autistic spectrum disorders*. London: Department of Health.

Department of Health (DoH) (2000) *The NHS plan*. London: DoH.

DoH (2001a) *The report of the public enquiry into children's heart surgery at the Bristol Royal Infirmary, 1984–1995: Learning from Bristol*. London: DoH.

DoH (2001b) *Seeking consent: Working with children*. London: DoH

DoH (2001c) *Consent – what you have a right to expect: A guide for children and young people*. London: DoH.

DoH (2001d) *Promoting the health of looked after children*. London: Stationery Office.

DoH (2002a) *Listening, hearing and responding: Core principles for the involvement of children and young people*. London: Stationery Office; www.dfes.gov.uk

DoH (2002b) *National standards for the provision of children's advocacy services*. London: Stationery Office.

DoH (2003a) *Listening, hearing and responding: Department of Health involving children and young people*. London: Stationery Office; www.dh.gov.uk

DoH (2003b) *Checklist of practice recommendations from the Victoria Climbié inquiry*. London: Stationery Office.

DoH (2003c) *NHS confidentiality code of practice*. London: Stationery Office.

DoH (2004a) *Getting the right start: National service framework for children, young people and maternity services*. London: DoH.

DoH (2004b) *The mental health and psychological well-being of children and young people*. London: Stationery Office.

DoH and DCSF (2009) *Healthy lives, brighter futures: The strategy for children and young people's health*. London: DoH.

DHSS (1974) *Report of the committee of inquiry into the care and supervision provided in relation to Maria Colwell*. London: DHSS. www.bopcris.ac.uk.

DHSS (1976) *Prevention and health: Everybody's business*. London: HMSO.

DHSS (1980) *The Black report. Inequalities in health. Report of a research working group*. London: DHSS.

DoH, Social Services and Public Safety (2003) *Seeking consent: Working with children*. London: Stationery Office.

Ding, S (2005) *Children's personal and social development*. Oxford: Blackwell.

Directgov (2008) *Compulsory learning age: Teenagers to stay in education or training until 18*. www.direct.gov.uk

Dowling, M (2005) *Young children's personal, social and emotional development*. 2nd edition. London: Paul Chapman.

Edwards, J and Fogelman, K. (1991) Active citizenship and young people. In K. Fogelman (ed.) *Citizenship in schools*. London: David Fulton.

Education Act 1996. www.opsi.gov.uk/ACTS/acts1996/uk

Education Act 2002. www.opsi.gov.uk/acts/acts2002/uk

Education and Skills Act 2008. www.opsi.gov.uk/acts/acts2008/uk

Education (Special Educational Needs) regulations 2001. www.opsi.gov.uk

Electoral Commission (2006) *Electoral registration in Great Britain and electoral registration in Northern Ireland*. www.electoralcommission.org.uk

Elfer, P, Goldschmeid, E and Selleck, D (2002) *Key persons in nurseries: Building relationships for quality provision*. London: NEYN.

Eliott, E and Watson, A (2000) Children's voices in health care planning. In Glasper, E and Ireland, L (eds) *Evidence-based child health care*. London: Macmillan.

Elliott, BE, Callery, P and Mould, J (2006) Chronic illness and the family. In Glasper, E and Richardson, J (eds) *A textbook of children's and young people's nursing*. London: Elsevier.

Engel, C and Gursky, E (2003) Management and interprofessional collaboration. In Leathard, A (ed.) *Interprofessional collaboration*. Hove and New York: Brunner-Routledge.

England, K (1996) Mothers, wives, workers: The everyday lives of working mother. In England, K (ed.) *Who will mind the baby?* London: Routledge.

Erickson, EH (1965) *Childhood and society*. 2nd edition. Harmondsworth: Penguin.

Erskine, T (2001) Assigning responsibilities to institutional moral agents: the case of states and quasi-states. *Ethics and International Affairs* 15(2), 67–85

Every Disabled Child Matters (2007) *If I could change one thing*. London: National Children's Bureau; www.edcm.org.uk

Family Law Reform Act (1969) www.opsi.gov.uk/RevisedStatutes

Farmer, E (1999) Holes in the safety net: The strengths and weaknesses of child protection procedures. *Child and Family Social Work*, 4: 293–302.

Farmer, JE, Marien, WE, Clark, MJ, Sherman, A and Selva, TJ (2004) Primary care supports for children with chronic health conditions: Identifying and predicting unmet family needs. *Journal of Pediatric Psychology*, 29: 355–67.

Fildes, V (1988). *Wet nursing: A history from antiquity to the present*. Oxford: Blackwell.

Finn, D (2003) *The 'employment first' welfare state: Lessons from the New Deal for young people*. Social Policy and Administration, 37 (7): 709–724. Available at: http://eprints.libr.port.ac.uk.

Fisher, HR (2001) The needs of parents with chronically sick children: A literature review. *Journal of Advanced Nursing*, 36(4): 600–607.

Fitzgerald, D and Kay, J (2008) *Working together in children services*. Abingdon: Routledge.

Fielding, M (2001) Students as radical agents of change. *Journal of Educational Change*, 2(2): 123–41.

Florian, L (1998) Inclusive practice: what, why and how? In Tilstone, C, Florian, L and Rose, R (eds) *Promoting inclusive*. London: Routledge/Falmer Press.

Foley, P, Roche, J and Tucker, S (2001) *Children in society*. Basingstoke: Palgrave Macmillan.

France, A (2007) *Understanding youth in late modernity*. Maidenhead: Open University Press.

Fraser, D (2003) *The evolution of the British welfare state*. 3rd edition, Basingstoke: Palgrave

Frost, N (2005) *Professionalism, partnership and join up thinking: A research review of front line working with children and families*. Totnes: Research in Practice.

General Medical Council (2007) *0–18 years: Guidance for all doctors*. London: GMC.

George, V and Miller, S (1994) *Social policy towards 2000: Squaring the welfare circle*. New York: Routledge.

Giddens, A (1998) *The third way: The renewal of social democracy*. Cambridge: Polity.

Gilchrist, R, Jeffs, T and Spence, J (eds) (2001) *Essays in the history of community and youth work*. Leicester: National Youth Agency.

Glasper, EA and Haggerty, REA (2006) The psychological preparation of children for hospitalisation. In Glasper, A and Richardson, J (eds) *A textbook of children's and young people's nursing*, London: Elsevier.

Glenny, G and Roaf, C (2008) *Multi-professional communication: Making systems work for children*. Maidenhead: McGraw-Hill.

Goleman, D (1995*) Emotional intelligence: Why it matters more than IQ*. London: Bantam.

Goleman, D (2005) *Emotional intelligence*. 10th anniversary edition. London: Bantam.

Gomez de la Cuesta, G, Humphrey, A and Baron-Cohen, S (2009) Evaluation of Lego™ therapy. www.autismresearch centre.com

Granberg, A, Bergbom-Endberg, I and Lundberg, D (1996) Intensive care syndrome: A literature review. *Intensive and Critical Care Nursing*, 12: 173–82.

Guggenheim, A and Fairbrother, JE (2005) A deficit in visits to the optometrist by preschool-age children: Implications for vision screening. *British Journal of Ophthalmology*, 89(2): 246–47.

Haiait, H, Bar-mor, G and Schobat, M (2003) The world of the child: A world of play even in hospital. *Pediatric Nursing*, 18(3): 209–14.

Hall, LJ and McGregor, JA (2000) A follow-up study of the peer relationship of children with disabilities in an inclusive school. *Journal of Special Education*, 34(3): 114–26.

Hantler, AM (2008) *How to nurture and enhance children's emotional development*. Cambridge: LDA.

Harden, J, Scott, S, Backett-Milburn, K and Jackson, S (2000) Can't talk, won't talk? Methodological issues in researching children. *Sociological Research Online*. 5 (2). www.socresonline.org.uk.

Hardy, B, Turrell, A and Wistow, G (1992) *Innovations in community care management*. Aldershot: Avebury.

Haringey Local Safeguarding Children Board (2008) *Haringey serious case review, November 2008: Child A.* www.haringey.gov.uk

Harrison, R and Wise, C (eds) (2005) *Working with young people*. London: Sage.

Hart, RA (1992) Children's participation: From tokenism to citizenship. Innocenti Essays No.4. UNICEF International Child Development Centre, Florence.

Hawton, K, Rodham, K, with Evans, E (2006) *By their own young hand: Deliberate self-harm and suicidal ideas in adolescents*. London: Jessica Kingsley.

Hay, MC, Cadigan, RJ, Khanna, D, Strthmann, C, Leiber, E et al. (2008) Prepared patients: Internet information seeking by new rheumatology patients. *Arthritis and Rheumatism*, 59: 575–82.

Hazel, N (1995) Elicitation techniques with young people. *Social Research Update*, 12, www.soc.surrey.ac.uk

Health and Social Care Act 2003. www.opsi.gov.uk

Hein, S (2007) *The innate potential model of emotional intelligence*. www.eqi.org

Herbert, M and Harper Dorton, KV (2001) *Working with children and their families*. London: Lyceum Books.

Holmes, J (2001) Youth and community work in the 70s: A missed opportunity? In Gilchrist, R, Jeffs, T and Spence, J (eds) *Essays in the history of community and youth work*. Leicester: Youth Work Press.

Honey, E, Leekam, S, Turner, M and McConachie, H (2006) Repetitive behaviour and play in typically developing children and children with Autistic Spectrum Disorders. *Journal of Autism and Developmental Disorders*, 37(6): 1107–15.

Hooton, S (2000) Promoting child and family health through empowerment. In Kerr, J (ed.) *Community health promotion: Challenges for practice*. London: Balliere-Tindall.

Hughes, B (2009) Letter from Minister of State Beverley Hughes to Martin Winter, mayor of Doncaster Council: response to the findings of the diagnostic review of Children's Services in the borough,12 March. www.dcsf.gov.uk

Human Rights Act (1998) www.hmso.gov.uk/acts/acts

Immigration and Asylum Act (1999) www.opsi.gov.uk/acts

Information Commission Office (2006) *Freedom of information Act Awareness Guidance No. 1*. www.ico.gov.uk

James, A (1998) Children health and illness. In Field, D and Taylor, S (eds) *Sociological perspectives on health, illness and healthcare*. London: Blackwell.

James, A, Jenks, C and Prout, A (1998) *Theorising childhood*. Cambridge: Polity Press.

Jary, D and Jary, J (2002) *Collins dictionary of sociology*. Glasgow Keil: Harper Collins.

Jordan, B (2006) *Social policy for the twenty-first century: New perspectives, big issues.* Cambridge: Polity Press.

Keil, S (2003) Survey of educational provision for blind and partially sighted children in England, Scotland and Wales in 2002. *British Journal of Visual Impairment*, 21: 93–7.

Kennedy, I (2001) *The inquiry into the management of care of children receiving complex heart surgery at the Bristol Royal Infirmary*. http://www.bristol-inquiry.org.uk

Keren, M, Feldman, R and Tyano, S (2001) Diagnoses and interactive patterns of infants referred to a community-based infant mental health clinic. *Journal of the American Academy of Child and Adolescent Psychiatry*, 40(1): 27–35.

Kerfoot, M (2001) Youth suicide and deliberate self harm. In Aggleton, P, Hurry, J and Warwick, I (eds) *Young people and mental health*. London: Wiley, p. 111.

Koshti-Richman, A (2008) Listening to parents and carers of children with disabilities. *Paediatric Nursing*, 20(7): 43–44.

Kumpulainen, K and Wray, D (2001) *Classroom interactions and social learning: From theory to practice*. London: Routledge.

Lam, KSL, Bodfish, JW and Piven, J (2008) Evidence for three subtypes of repetitive behavior in autism that differ in familiality and association with other symptoms. *Journal of Child Psychology and Psychiatry*, 49(11): 1193–1200.

Laming, Lord (2003) *The Victoria Climbié inquiry report.Cm5730*. London: Stationery Office; www.victoria-Climbié-inquiry.org.uk

Laming, Lord (2009) *The protection of children in England: A progress report*. London: Stationery Office.

Lancaster, YP (2006) *RAMPS: a framework for listening to children*. London: Day Care Trust.

Lansdown, R (1998) Communicating with children. In Goldman, A (ed.) *Care of the dying child*. Oxford: Oxford University Press.

Layard, R and Dunn, J (2009) *A good childhood: Searching for values in a competitive age*. London: Children's Society.

Learning and Skills Act 2000. www.opsi.gov.uk/Acts

Leinster-Mackay, DP (1984) *The rise of the English prep. school*. London: Falmer Press.

Lewington, W, Clipson, C, for the Independent Advocacy Commission (IAC) (2001) *Advocating for equality*. London: Scope.

Lewis, A (1995) *Children's understandings of disability*. London: Routledge.

Lewis, A (2002) Accessing, through research interviews, the views of children with difficulties in learning. *Support for Learning*, 17(3): 110–16.

Lindley, B and Richards, M (2002) *Protocol on advice and advocacy for parents (child protection)*. London: Centre for Family Research.

Local Government Act 2000. www.opsi.gov.uk/Acts

Lombard, D (2009) *Vale of Glamorgan Council launches inquiry into placement of teenager: Community Care*. www.communitycare.co.uk

MacAskill, K (2009) *Criminal Justice and Licensing (Scotland) Bill (SP Bill 24)*, 9 March. www.scottish.parliament.uk

MacBeath, J, Demetriou, H, Rudduck, J and Myers, K (2003) *Consulting pupils: A toolkit for teachers*. Cambridge: Pearson Education.

MacDonald, R and Marsh, J (2005) *Disconnected youth? Growing up in Britain's Poor Neighbourhoods*. Basingstoke: Palgrave Macmillan.

McCormack, B (2004) Person-centredness in gerontological nursing: an overview of the literature. *Journal of Clinical Nursing*, 13 (suppl.): 31–8.

Marchant, R and Cross, M (2002) *How it is: An image vocabulary for children about feelings, rights and safety, personal care and sexuality*. London: NSPCC and Triangle. www.howitis.org.uk

Markus, J, Mundy, P, Morales, M, Delgado, CEF and Yale, M (2000) Individual differences in infant skills as predictors of childcare-giver joint attention and language. *Social Development*, 9(3): 302–15.

Marsen, S (2006) *Communication studies*. Basingstoke: Palgrave Macmillan.

Maslow, AH (1998) *Towards a psychology of being*. 3rd edition. London: Wiley.

Martinic, M and Measham, F (2008) *Swimming with crocodiles: The culture of extreme drinking* (International Centre for Alcohol Policies Series on Alcohol in Society). London: Routledge.

Marvin, RS and Brittner, PA (1995) Classification system for parental caregiving patterns in the preschool strange situation, University of Virginia.

Masters, K (2005) *Role development in professional nursing practice*. Sudbury: Jones and Bartlett.

Mathews, J (2006) Communicating with children and their families. In Glasper, A and Richardson, J (eds) *A textbook of children's and young people's nursing*. London: Elsevier.

Mathisen, L and Butterworth, D (2001) The role of play in hospitalisation of young children. *Neonatal, Pediatric and Child Health Nursing*, 4(3): 23–26.

Maud, V (2002) *Stress and depression in children and teenagers (overcoming common problems)*. London: Sheldon Press.

Mauthner, M (1997) Methodological aspects of collecting data from children: Lessons from three research projects. *Children and Society*, 11(1): 16–28.

Mayall, B (2001) Conversations with children: Working with generational issues. In Christensen, P and James, A (eds), *Research with children – perspectives and practices*. London: Routledge/Falmer Press.

McCormack, B. (2001) *Negotiating partnerships with older people: A person-centred approach*. Aldershot: Ashgate.

McGee, F and Barn, G (2007) *Training for change: Emerging impact of the Ready Steady Change and other participation training materials*. London: CRAE.

McGrath, P and Huff, N (2001) 'What is it?' Findings on preschoolers' responses to play with medical equipment. *Child Care, Health and Development*, 27(5): 451–462.

McMurray, I, Connolly, H, Preston-Shoot, M and Wigley, V (2008) Constructing resilience: Social workers' understandings and practice. *Health Society Care Community*, 16(3): 299–309.

McLaughlan, B (2009) *Screening for vision defects can play a vital part in identifying potential sight problems in children: Do health authorities recognise the need for such a service?* 23 March. www.vision2020uk.org.uk

McNamara, C, Hay P, Katsikitis, M and Chur-Hansen, A (2008) Emotional responses to food, body dissatisfaction and other eating disorder features in children, adolescents and young adults. *Appetite*, 50(1): 102–109.

Meads, G and Ashcroft, J (2005) *The case for interprofessional collaboration*. Oxford: Blackwell.

Medicines and Healthcare Products Regulatory Body (MHRA) (2009). *Paracetamol overdose*. www.mhra.gov.uk

Mehrabian, A (1971) *Silent messages*. Belmont, CA: Wadsworth.

MENCAP (2004) *Mencap advocacy strategy*. London: MENCAP.

MENCAP (2007) *Don't stick it, stop it!* London: Mencap; www.dontstickit.org.uk

Mental Capacity Act (2005). www.opsi.gov.uk/acts/acts

Mental Health Foundation (2006) *Truth hurts: Report of the national inquiry into self-harm among young people*. London: MHF.

Messiou, K (2002) Marginalisation in primary schools: Listening to children's voices. *Support for Learning*, 17(3): 117–21.

Messiou, K (2003) *Conversations with children: A pathway towards understanding marginalisation and inclusive education*. Manchester: University of Manchester. [Unpublished PhD thesis]

Messiou, K (2006a) Conversations with children: Making sense of marginalisation in primary school settings. *European Journal of Special Needs Education*, 21(1): 39–54.

Messiou, K (2006b) Understanding marginalisation in education: The voice of children. *European Journal of Psychology of Education (Special Issue)*, 21(3): 305–18.

Messiou, K (2008) Encouraging children to think in more inclusive ways. *British Journal of Special Needs Education*, 35(1): 26–32.

Midgley, J, Tracy, M and Livermore, M (2009) *Social science: The handbook of social policy*. Thousand Oaks, CA: Sage.

Millar, S and Scott, J (2003) What is augmentative and alternative communication? An introduction. In Communication Aids for Language and Learning and the Scottish Executive Education Department. *Augmentative communication in practice: An introduction*; callcentre.education.ed.ac.uk.

Miller, C and Freeman, M (2003) Clinical teamwork: The impact of policy on collaborative practice. In Leathard, A (ed.), *Interprofessional collaboration*. Hove and New York: Brunner-Routledge.

Mills, R (2000) Perspectives of childhood. In Mill, J and Mills, R (eds) *Childhood studies: A reader in perspectives of childhood*. London: Routledge.

Mittler, P (2000) *Working towards inclusive education: Social contexts*. London: David Fulton.

Mizen, P (2004) *The changing state of youth*. Basingstoke: Palgrave.

Morris, J (ed.) (2006) *Safeguarding disabled children: A resource for local safeguarding children boards*. London: Department for Education and Skills.

Moreno, JL (1934) *Who shall survive?* New York: Beacon House.

Morrow, V and Richards, M (1996) The ethics of social research with children: An overview. *Children and Society*, 10 (2): 90–105.

Murray, C (1984) *Losing ground: American social policy. 1950–1980*, New York: Basic Books.

Muschamp, Y M, Naidoo, R (2002) A decent education for all? In Powell, M (ed.), *Evaluating New Labour's welfare reforms*. Bristol: Policy Press, 145–66.

National Autistic Society (2002) Do children with autistic spectrum disorder have a special relationship with Thomas the Tank Engine, and if so, why? London: NAS; www.nas.org.uk

National Autistic Society (2003) *Approaches to autism: An easy to use guide to many and varied approaches to autism.* 5th edition. London: National Autistic Society.

National Health Service Act 1977. www.opsi.gov.uk

National Institute for Clinical Excellence (NICE) (2004a) *Eating disorders: core interventions in the treatment and management of anorexia nervosa, bulimia nervosa and related eating disorders. Clinical Guideline 9*. London: NICE.

NICE (2004b) *Self harm: The short-term physical and psychological management and secondary prevention of self harm in primary and secondary care*. London: NICE.

NICE (2006) *Obesity guidance on the prevention, identification, assessment and management of overweight and obesity in adults and children*. London: NICE.

National Working Group on Child Protection and Disability (2003) *It doesn't happen to disabled children: Child protection and disabled children. Report of the National Working Group on Child Protection and Disability*. London: NSPCC.

Noyes, J (2000) Enabling young 'ventilator dependent' people to express their views and experiences of their care in hospital. *Journal of Advanced Nursing*, I31(5): 1206–1215.

NSPCC (2007) *Childline: A series of reports on issues facing children today. Calls to ChildLine about depression and mental health*. London: NSPCC.

NSPCC (2008) *NSPCC evidence to Lord Laming's review of child protection*. December. www.nspcc.org.uk

NSPCC (2009) *NSPCC response to the Child and Adolescent Mental Health Services (CAMHS) national review 2008: Call for evidence*, 4 April. www.nspcc.org.uk

Office for National Statistics (2005) *Survey of the mental health of children and young people in Great Britain, 2004*. London: ONS.

Ofsted (1999) *Principles into practice: Effective education for pupils with emotional and behavioural difficulties*. London: Stationery Office.

O'Hagan, K (2006) *Identifying emotional and psychological abuse: A guide for childcare professionals*. Maidenhead: Open University Press.

O'Kane, C (2000) The development of participatory techniques: Facilitating children's views about decisions which affect them. In Christensen, P and James, A (eds) *Research with children: Perspectives and practices*. London: Routledge/Falmer Press.

Oliver, C, Knight, A and Candappa, M (2006) *A summary of the key findings of the first national study of children's advocacy in England*, prepared for the Department of Health and the DfEs. London: University of London.

Parliamentary Office of Science and Technology (2005) *Binge drinking and public health*. Number 244, www.parliament.uk

Parton, N (1985) *The politics of child abuse*. London, Macmillan.

Petrie, P (1997) *Communicating with children and adults: Interpersonal skills for early years and play work*. London: Edward Arnold.

Pietroni, PC (1992) Towards reflective practice – the languages of health and social care', *Journal of Interprofessional Care* (6)1: 7–16.

Pilcher, J and Wagg, S (1996) Introduction: Thatcher's children? In Pilcher, J and Wagg, S *Thatcher's children? Politics, childhood and society in the 1980s and 1990s*. London: Falmer Press.

Playfor, S Thomas, D and Choonara, I (2000) Recollections of children following intensive care. *Archives of Disease in Childhood*, 83: 445–448.

Prior, V (2006) *Understanding attachment and attachment disorders: Theory, evidence and practice*. London: Jessica Kingsley.

Protection of Children Act (1999) www.opsi.gov.uk

Scottish Law Commission (2001) *Discussion paper (No 115) on the age of criminal responsibility*. www.scotlawcom.gov.uk

Sexual Offences Act (2003). www.opsi.gov.uk/acts

Prout, A and James, A (1990) Introduction. In James, A and Prout, A (eds) *Constructing and reconstructing childhood: contemporary issues in the sociological study of childhood*. London: Falmer Press.

Punch, S. (2002) Interviewing strategies with young people: the 'secret box' stimulus material and task-based activities. *Children and Society*, 16(1): 45–56.

Qvortrup, J (1994). Childhood matters: An introduction. In Qvortrup, J, Bardy, M, Sgritta, G and Wintersberger, H (eds) *Childhood matters: social theory, practice and politics*. Aldershot: Avebury.

Rahi, JS and Cable, N (2003) Severe sight problems and blindness in children in the UK. *Lancet*, 362: 1359–65.

Rassini, M et al. (2004) Developing a computer game to prepare children for surgery. *AORN*, 80(6): 1095–2006.

Rethink (2009) *Depression in children*. www.rethink.org

Roberts, H (2000) Listening to children: And hearing them. In Christensen, P and James, A (eds) *Research with children: Perspectives and practices*. London: RoutledgeFalmer.

Roberts, K (2002) Exploring participation: Older people on discharge from hospital. *Journal of Advanced Nursing*, 40 (4): 413–20.

Robbins, A (2002) How does total communication affect cochlear implant performance in children? Paper presented at the 4th ACFOS International Conference, 'The impact of scientific advances on the education of deaf children', Paris.

Robinson, JR (2002) Attachment problems and disorders in infants and young children: Identification, assessment and intervention. *Infants and Young Children*, 14(4): 6–18.

Rogers, C (1961) *On becoming a person*. Boston: Houghton Mifflin.

Rose, R and Shevlin, M (2004) Encouraging voices: Listening to young people who have been marginalised. *Support for Learning*, 19(4): 155–61.

Rosengren, K (2000) *Communication: An introduction*. London: Sage.

Royal College of General Practitioners (2000) *Confidentiality and young people. Improving teenagers' uptake of sexual and other health advice: A tool-kit for general practice, primary care groups and trusts*. London: RCGP

Royal College of Paediatrics and Child Health (2009) Children and young people's participation. Newsletter, Spring, pp5. http://www.rcpch.ac.uk/Publications/Newsletter-and-Annual-Report

Royal College of Psychiatrists (2004) *Deliberate self harm in young people*. 3rd edition. www.rcpsych.ac.uk

Royal National Institute for the Blind (RNIB) (2008) *Statistics: Numbers of people with sight problems by age group in the UK*. London. RNIB; www.rnib.org.uk

Royal National Institute for the Deaf (RNID) (2005) *Facts and figures on deafness and tinnitus*. www.rnid.org.uk

RNID (2007) *Starting to sign*. 4th edition. London: RNID.

RNID (2009) *Sign language: What it is and how you can learn it*. London: RNID; www.rnid.org.uk

Rudduck, J and Flutter, J (2000) Pupil participation and pupil perspective: Carving a new order of experience. *Cambridge Journal of Education*, 30 (1): 75–89.

Rummery, K and Glendinning, C (2000) *Primary care and social services: Developing new partnerships for older people*. Oxford: Radcliffe Medical Press

Rutter, M (1981) *Maternal deprivation reassessed*. Harmondsworth: Penguin.

Shin, H and White-Traut, R (2005) Nurse–child interaction on an inpatient paediatric unit. *Journal of Advanced Nursing*, 52(1): 56–62.

Rutter, M and Taylor, E (eds) (2002) *Child and adolescent psychiatry*. 4th edition. London: Blackwell.

Santrock, JW (2007) *Child development*. London: McGraw-Hill.

Scope (2009) *Supporting communication through AAC. Module 9. Children and adults with profound and multiple learning difficulties*. London: Scope; www.scope.org.uk

Scott, A, Shaw, M and Joughin, C (eds) (2001) *Finding the evidence: A gateway to the literature in child and adolescent mental health*. 2nd edition. London: Gaskell.

SenseScotland (2008) *About deafblindness: An overview*. Glasgow: SenseScotland; www.sensescotland.org.uk

Simons, J and Roberson, E (2002) Poor communication and knowledge deficits: Obstacles to effective management of children's postoperative pain. *Journal of Advanced Nursing*, 40(1): 78–86.

Sisson, R (1990) Effects of auditory stimuli on comatose patients with head injury. *Heart and Lung*, 19(4): 373–378.

Skuse, T and Ward, H (2003) *The developing world of the child*. London: Jessica Kingsley.

Smart, B (2003) *Economy, culture and society: A sociological critique of neo-liberalism*. Buckingham: Open University.

Smith, L and Callery, P (2005) Children's accounts of their pre-operative information needs. *Journal of Clinical Nursing*, 14(2): 230–38.

Social Exclusion Unit (2006) *Reaching out: An action plan on social exclusion*. London: Cabinet Office; www.cabinet office.gov.uk

Spender, Q, Salt, N, Dorkins, J, Kendrick, T and Hill, P (2001) *Child mental health in primary care*. Abingdon: Radcliffe Medical.

Spiker, P (2008) *Models of welfare*. Available at http://www2.rgu.ac.uk.

Spiker, P (2008) *The United Kingdom: The welfare state*. Available at http://www2.rgu.ac.uk.

Stevens, R (2008) *Erik H Erikson: Explorer of identity and the life cycle (mind shapers)*. London: Palgrave Macmillan.

Sutherland, T (2003) Comparison of hospital and home base preparation for cardiac surgery. *Paediatric Nursing*, 15(5): 13–16.

Swallow, VM and Jacoby, A (2001) Mothers' evolving relationships with doctors and nurses during the chronic childhood illness trajectory. *Journal of Advanced Nursing*, 36(6): 755–64.

Swanwick, R and Tsverik, I (2007) The role of sign language for deaf children with cochlear implants: Good practice in sign bilingual settings. *Deafness and Education International*, 9(4): 214–231.

Stevenson-Hinde, J and Versheuren, K (2002) Attachment in childhood. In Smith, PK and Hart, CH (2002) *Blackwell handbook of childhood social development*. Oxford. Blackwell, Chapter 10.

Talge, NM, Donzella, B and Gunnar, MR (2008) Fearful temperament and stress reactivity among pre-school children. *Infant and Child Development*, 17(4): 427–45.

Tates, K, Meeuwesen, L and Bensing, J (2002) 'I've come for his throat': Roles and identities in doctor–parent–child communication. *Child: Care, Health and Development*, 28: 109–16.

Tattooing of Minors Act (1969). www.opsi.gov.uk

Thatcher, M (1987) Interview with *Women's Own Magazine*, October 31st.

Theunissen, N and Tates, K (2004) Models and theories in studies on educating and counseling children about physical health: A systematic review. *Patient Education and Counseling*, 55(3): 316–30.

Thomas, N and O' Kane, C (1998) The ethics of participatory research with children. *Children and Society*, 12(5): 336–48.

Thomson, P (2008) *Doing visual research with children and young people*. London: Routledge.

Thon, A and Ullrich, G (2008) Information needs in parents of children with a rheumatic disease. *Child: Care, Health and Development*, 35(1): 41–7.

Trapolini, T, Ungerer, JA and McMahon, CA (2007) Maternal depression and children's attachment representations during the preschool years. *British Journal of Developmental Psychology*, 25: 247–61.

Trevarthen, C and Aitken, KJ (2003) Infant intersubjectivity: Research, theory, and clinical applications. *Journal of Child Psychology and Psychiatry*, 42(1): 3–48.

Tunstall, J and Allnock, D (2007) *Understanding the contribution of Sure Start local programes to the task of safeguarding children's welfare*. London: Stationery Office.

Tutt, R, Powell, S and Thornton, M (2006) Educational approaches in autism: What we know about what we do. *Educational Psychology in Practice*, 22 (1): 69–81.

Weaving, LS, Ellaway, CJ, Gecz, J and Christodoulou, J (2005) Retts syndrome: Clinical review and genetic update. *Journal of Medical Genetics*, 42: 1–7.

Williams, JG, Higgins, JPT and Brayne, CEG (2006) Systematic review of prevalence studies of autism spectrum disorders. *Archives of Disease in Childhood*, 91(1): 8–15.

United Nations Convention on the Rights of the Child (1989). www.unicef.org

United Nations Committee on the Rights of the Child (2008) 49th session: Consideration of reports submitted by state parties under Article 44 of the Convention, Great Britain and Northern Ireland. www2.ohchr.org

UNICEF (2009) *A summary of the rights under the Convention on the Rights of the Child (1989)*. www.unicef.org

Vacik, HD, Nagy, MC and Jessee, PO (2001) Children's understanding of illness: Students' assessments. *Journal of Pediatric Nursing*, 16(6): 429–37.

Valuing People Support Team (2004) *Local planning for advocacy*. London: DoH.

Vanclay, L (2003) Supporting families: An interprofessional approach? In Leathard, A (ed.) *Interprofessional collaboration*. Hove and New York: Brunner-Routledge.

Vlachou, AD (1997) *Struggles for inclusive education*. Buckingham: Open University Press.

Waterhouse, R (2000) *Lost in care: Report of the tribunal of inquiry into the abuse of children in care in the former county council areas of Gwynedd and Clwyd since 1974*. London: Stationery Office.

Wheeler, R (2006) Gillick or Fraser? A plea for consistency over competence in children. *British Medical Journal*, 332: 807.

Widgit Symbols © Widgit Software (2009) www.widgit.com used by Marchant, R and Cross, M (2002) How it is. An image vocabulary for children about: feelings, rights and safety, personal care and sexuality. London: NSPCC and Triangle. www.howitis.org.uk

Williams, PDW, Williams, AR, Graff, JC et al. (2003) A community-based intervention for siblings and parents of children with chronic illness or disability. *Journal of Pediatrics*, 142(3): 386–393.

Wolfer, JA and Visintainer, MA (1975) Pediatric surgical patients' and parents' stress responses and adjustment as a function of psychological preparation and stress point nursing care. *Nursing Research*, 24: 244–255.

World Health Organisation (2000) *Elimination of avoidable visual disability due to refractive errors* (WHO/PBL/00.79), Vision 2020. www.v2020.org

Wyld, N (2002) *Your voice, your choice: A guide for children and young people about the national advocacy standards*. London: Voice for the Child in Care.

Young, B, Dixon-Woods, M, Findlay, M and Heney, D (2002) Parenting in crisis: Conceptualising mothers of children with cancer. *Social Science and Medicine*, 55: 1835–47.

Zandt, F, Prior, M and Kyrios, M (2007) Repetitive behaviour in children with high functioning autism and obsessive compulsive disorder. *Journal of Autism and Developmental Disorders*, 37(2): 251–9.

Zelman, J, Cassano, M, Perry Parrish, C and Stegall, S (2006) Emotional regulation in children and adolescents. *Journal of Developmental and Behavioral Pediatrics*, 27(2): 155–168.

Useful websites

http://www.11million.org.uk
www.1voice.info
http://www.afasic.org.uk
www.b-eat.co.uk/Home
www.communicationmatters.org.uk
www.dh.gov.uk
www.edcm.org.uk/Page.asp
www.howitis.org.uk
www.ican.org.uk/TalkingPoint/Home.aspx
www.makaton.org
www.mentalhealth.org.uk
www.mhf.org.uk
www.mind.org.uk
www.nelh.nhs.uk
www.nshn.org.uk
www.rnib.org.uk
www.rnid.org.uk
www.rcpsych.ac.uk/info
www.scope.org.uk/education/aac.php
www.selfharmalliance.org.uk
www.selfharm.org.uk
www.sense.org.uk
www.thetransporters.com
www.Youngminds.org.uk
www.actionforchildren.org.uk
www.barnardos.org.uk
www.bichard.inquiry.org
www.bristol-inquiry.org.uk
www.childrenslawcentre.org

www.crae.org.uk
www.edcm.org.uk
www.everychildmatters.gov.uk
www.mencap.org.uk
www.ncb.org.uk
www.nspcc.org.uk/inform
www.nyas.net/aboutus.html
www.opsi.gov.uk/Acts
www.savethechildren.org.uk
www.rights4me.org
www.unicef.org
www.victoria-climbie-inquiry.org.uk/

Index